PETER COX

THE DREAM IS EVERYTHING

DEDICATION

To my beautiful wife Debbie and two magnificent boys Dane & Jarrod who inspire me to be the best I can be. I love them with all my heart.

This book is to thank my family for their love, belief, patience and joy they create. They are my dream and drive me on to bigger and bigger dreams.

To my parents Brian & Claire who brought me from England to Australia in 1965 when I was two years old hoping my dreams would come true. My father is somebody I have always admired and respected for his values and his integrity.

ACKNOWLEDGEMENTS

The dream becomes a nightmare when the family unit falls apart. The most important person in my life is my wife Debbie who took a chance with me December 1985. This book is a team effort due to the tremendous wisdom and insight we have as partners in life over the last sixteen and a half years.

My two beautiful sons Dane and Jarrod create the drive inside me to keep on chasing the next dream because they are the future and deserve a dream life.

It only takes one person to believe in you. One of my closest friends Werner Clarey shared my vision with this book December 2000 and then expanded it due to his belief in me, and the incredible entrepreneurial skills he possesses.

A special thanks to Lisa Clarey and Rob Wilson for partnering with the vision Werner Clarey had with this book and helped me formulate the vision and create the right strategies to launch this book globally.

To a new friend Craig Heilmann for catching the vision and doing the research to create this book in Auckland, New Zealand.

There are giants in this world. They create the vision and they impact the world by enabling others to have their dreams come true.

I have been able to see farther by standing on the shoulders of Jim and Nancy Dornan who are my personal mentors in Atlanta/Georgia. Jim and Nancy created an opportunity globally for Debbie and I to utilise and make our dreams come true.

This book would not be possible without their vision and commitment to their dreams and other people's dreams.

Without the guidance, expertise and encouragement from the C.E.O of Network 21 globally – Jeff Neuber, this book of mine would have taken so much longer. Thanks for your wisdom Jeff in the finer details of creating a book.

For ten years we have had a personal assistant Christine Chandler watch the dream become a reality. Starting from our office in a fibro garage to ten plus countries internationally Christine has been dedicated, loyal, patient, encouraging and one hundred percent loving and committed to our vision and dreams.

To our general manager Alex Wah Day for professionally structuring the financial side of our company and providing third party advice as a "No Man" to keep the dream moving forward for all of us.

To the global leadership team we are proud to lead and mentor who have been loyal and patient with me, as I have made the necessary changes to be the best leader that I can be. There are too many leaders to mention but they know who they are and this book is the result of their fight for wanting freedom and a better life.

To my closest personal friends Craig, Robert, John, Nick, Adam, Greg and Werner. For accepting my passion and understanding my heart which drives me towards making the dream a reality.

Thank you.

Introduction

A very influential Australian once told me that I am a guy with a lot of passion. So this book comes to you from someone with a passion: a simple bloke from the back streets of Campbelltown, born to immigrant parents from Palmers Green, North London, England.

I say that up front, lest at the outset you think here's another book by someone who was destined for success. Believe me, I wasn't. I was raised in redbrick utopia—surrounded by 'fibros'—of the sort poorer Australians are renowned for in Western Sydney.

The one very important thing, among many, that I inherited from my parents was the will to win. Dad was a champion boxer and cricketer. Born in Mumbai, India, in 1935, he became a schoolboy boxing-champion, pulverising men from the Indian army. Between 1953 and 1956, my father served in the British army, for whom he played field hockey.

Having moved to Hong Kong with the army, my father met my mother, also a great hockey player, and represented Hong Kong in both hockey and swimming. My dad also paired with a lady to become the British colony's mixed doubles table-tennis champion. My mother was born in Shanghai, China, of French descent, during the French Concession and lived there from 1936-46, her family enduring the brutal, World War II Japanese invasion and bombing, before hastily fleeing to Hong Kong with the onset of Mao's Revolution.

In 1956, upon his return to England, my father embarked upon his dream of a professional cricketing career, trialing as a County cricket all-rounder—an opening batsman and fast bowler—until a lack of funds and sponsorship, together with the bitter bias attached to his colonial upbringing, crushed his dream of playing for England. Boy, how that must have hurt dad, and yet, funnily, he never told me his story until one day, in my childhood, along with my best friend Craig Bennison, we watched my father play a game of A-grade cricket, and stared open mouthed as he ripped apart the bowling with the bat (scoring 100 plus) and took seven for not many (including a hat trick) with the ball. While dad was batting, 'Benno' and I spent all day running to the boundary with glee throwing the ball back to the opposition players. I was chuffed. Ironically, at that time, my dad hadn't played cricket probably for 20 years. It was then I realised just how talented my dad was, and what, perhaps, he could have been.

My parents' successful sporting legacy instilled in me a fierce competitive streak and a passion for winning that has stood me in good stead throughout my life. Still, I was not guaranteed success. I first had to get a dream and then learn how to fight for it.

In this book you will discover how, with the inspiration my dream afforded, the belief my wife has poured out and the passion I reached inside to find, I have conquered obstacles too great and too many to number. As I tell you my own story, it is my desire that you, too, will master the essential lessons, take hold of the required skills and find the inner belief so needed to fulfill the highest goals, dreams and aspirations you have for your life.

I write this book today because I have lived it—for seventeen years now—and because I believe with all my heart that no matter where you stand today, no matter what cards you think you have been dealt, good or bad, you can still learn to play a winning hand.

So, here's a little of my story just to wet your appetite.

I grew up, working class, in Campbelltown—in Sydney's west. Campbelltown was a tough neighbourhood. I well remember a certain pair of brothers who used to wait for me after school on a certain lane way to beat the snot out of me. I knew if I didn't get to that lane before they did, I would become their personal punching bag. Consequently, my early school days were tied up with massive fear and terror. And it didn't stop there, because in my first few days at High School the local tough guy decided he didn't like the look of me. Word spread like wildfire that he had picked 'Coxy' for his punching bag. So, when the news reached my dad, he took me out to the backyard, thrust a pair of gloves onto my hands, laced them up rather tightly and said, 'Right, son, you're going to have to learn to defend yourself.'

I stood there uncertain and trembling while he told me to be sure that if I hit, to hit first and to hit hard. 'What do you mean by that?' I timidly asked. Wrong question! Wham! My dad hit me with a sledgehammer right hook smashing me clean on the nose.

Come eight o'clock Monday morning, my father had me mentally and physically prepared for the fight. Two or three hundred kids had gathered in the quadrangle like jackals around a carcass. I walked into the quad and I didn't even give him time to shape up before I clocked him under the right eye. The next thing I remember is sitting on top of him pounding my fists into him, one after the other—into his face, his chin, his nose, whatever, until a teacher lifted me off and dragged me to the principal's office for six of the best (the cane).

My fight had been motivated by fear, but when I got back to the classroom, I had respect. The local tough guy never bothered me again.

I had a big mouth at school, which got me into a lot of trouble. I just couldn't shut up. I talked and talked and talked. Anyone who sat next to me in class instantly failed. It was called the Cox-bell curve. Anyone seated near me ranked dead last at the bottom of the curve. But they always had company: I never excelled at school, either. Except in sports.

At the age of 13, I decided to enter the school cross-country championships. After several weeks of training, running up steep hills with a heavy pack on my shoulders by way of getting myself in shape, I won the school champs; then the area champs; and went on to finish eighth in New South Wales, distinguishing myself with a colourful spit-vomit as I crossed over the finish line. I had only trained for eight weeks, but I had learned a few lessons about discipline and experienced pain and loneliness—I ran on my own every night, to prepare for the event. Indeed, that was the first time in my life I had ever disciplined myself to achieve anything.

My friends at High School were not the associates likely to set me on a good course in life. The most honest people I knew there shoplifted. For kicks, the antisocial ones hotwired other people's cars. The rest toted guns, and sharpened Ginsu knives on their nipple rings. My school was surrounded by Housing Commission homes in every direction, homes where hopelessness, deprivation and hardship were as common as vegemite sandwiches elsewhere. Thus, I spent many of my formative years passing time with kids from very dysfunctional family backgrounds who had no hope, unless they could find a dream to do something extraordinary and change their lives.

After my parents pulled me out of that particular Western-Sydney High School, I attended a prestigious Grammar school in Strathfield, which meant leaving Campbelltown at 6.00 a.m. every day to catch the trains to Summer Hill and then to Strathfield. I got home in the evening about 6.00 p.m. (After a year or so our family moved south to Cronulla.)

This was a lonely time. The trek from the moral wilderness of my old high school to the prickly formality of the Anglican Grammar School scene represented quite a leap. I wasn't exactly adored at my new home when I first arrived, and I hated the sterility the rules and disciplines engendered.

I distinguished myself at Grammar school by missing morning roll 30 times in a row—hanging out with the cool and tough 'surfie' guys—before I got my first Saturday detention. Believe it or not, I was good enough to think of a different excuse for each day of lateness. In the end, I lasted only two years, before blowing my cover.

For two years my parents and I had worked tirelessly to hide my sporting prowess from the school so that on weekends I could play top-level soccer. We told the school I had to work, because we were a poor family from Campbelltown and struggled to meet the fees. Little did they know, however, I was playing soccer. Mine was a rugby school and their soccer set up was garbage; if the school had known I could play soccer, they would have shackled me into their two-bit system, much to my game's detriment.

In a stupid moment with friends I bet them $5 each that I could outrun the school champion. I hadn't trained at all, but I knew the school champion's times, and I was more than confident that I could take him. (The last 500m, however, I did it pretty tough —especially after that B&H special filter I puffed just before the race started.)

I was cocky back then (little has changed), so I told the school champion that I would give him a 30m start; when the gun went everyone took off, but I just stood there. I still beat that laggard by 500 metres.

My headmaster and sports master were waiting at the finish line, and they took me back to the headmaster's office to convince me to join an Anglican boarding school, where I could train and compete in the private school (CAS) championships. That was the sort of stuff (that was how I saw things then) that got the Anglican school system in a palpable frenzy—someone who could win them some prestige at some other elite school's expense.

So naturally, I threw a fit in the Headmaster's office, overturning tables and upending chairs in my rage and frustration. I had blown my cover for a lousy 50 bucks. I rang mum and dad and said, 'You better come and get me!' And they came right away.

That was the end of my Grammar school days and I found myself enrolled on the following Monday at a government high school in the south of Sydney.

Of course, by this time my real dream was starting to take shape—women. And boy what shape, too! The testosterone was flowing. The hormones were starting to become female-seeking missiles.

Aside from girls, however, there were other issues to confront. Boy, did I have a tough time when I got to my new school! There were two guys in particular who wanted to use my face for tap-dance lessons; one of them, a burly carrot-top, eventually became a great friend. The perception was that coming from an Anglican Grammar, I was too good for the fine folks of the Sutherland shire, and it is fair to say that the tough carrot-top, his brother and friends didn't take an immediate shine to me.

Still, I bravely decided to try to get in with the 'right crowd'. My approaches were rebuffed. There was a simple tradition at this school: the last guy holding the Rugby League ball when the lunch bell rang would get belted by every other bloke on the field. Carrot-top made sure that in my first week, when the lunch bell rang, I was dished the ball. Bang ... crash ... kaboom ... Welcome to Woolooware—love, the boys!

I eventually made friends with these guys by going on a camping trip to Stanwell Top, south of Sydney, and drinking a case of beer by myself. That rather bizarre rite of passage got me in the good books with the boys and assured my acceptance with the 'in' crowd. Anyone who could drink that much beer, the boys reasoned, couldn't be all bad.

That Sutherland shire government high school represented a typical Aussie education—majoring in booze, girls and parties, and with a double major in time wasting! It was the best time of my school career. I even became 'cool', moving through the ranks to become something of a lad, and even, may I add, a ladies' man.

From high school in Sutherland, I went to the New South Wales Institute of Technology, where I chiselled out a niche market in doing as little as possible, but working my way to a degree in business with a major in marketing. (I pitied any firm who would let me market their products, however, because I usually copied my work from the girls in my classes.) There was no way I would have taken on economics, because then I would have had to work too hard, so I went after marketing instead. That's how little ambition I actually possessed in those days. I was almost totally directionless.

There at university, of course, I explored, to the fullest possible extent, what I thought might be my subsequent two major life passions—women (and more women) and booze. I took a big liking to both, investing most of my time, energy and money on them.

My home life at this time was rather unstable. I moved out of home at 18 and, as many young people with no understanding of economics do, moved back home at 19. Only to move out again at 20 after a financial windfall, and back home again at 21 after a major investment reversal I hadn't planned for—it was called rent! (Like most youth, money seemed to find a way to slip through my fingers and I had no real idea how to get ahead in life.) Then, after another minor windfall, I bolted out from home for good.

Like so many young Australians, I was not happy at home for too many reasons to go into fully. Suffice it to say, home was tumultuous — particularly my relationship with my beloved mother who I think struggled to make the shift from mothering a boy to an adult friendship with a grown up male. Sometimes, I felt very frustrated, and exposed my anger in the wrong places. (One soccer season with the Cronulla Seagulls, when I was 19, I played 28 games and received 18 yellow cards for foul play—I was shooting for some kind of angry-guy record). I have since learned to channel my emotions into productive work, and that has helped me attain the success you will read about in this book.

My father also struggled with my university study habits. One night, after being told by him to stay home and study, I sneaked out down the drainpipe for a night of merriment and smuggled myself—quietly enough I thought—back into the house at 3.00

a.m. Drunk, stumbling and bumbling blindly, with my ears ringing and the dog barking, and for some queer and inexplicable reason repeatedly shushing myself, suddenly I saw a naked man—gigantic—like an avenging angel wreathed by the glimmering moonbeams of the hall skylight—my father—and I took a double take. 'I thought I told you not to go to the pub!' Bam. He hit me in the shoulder with his fist. Down I went (dad had given it everything he had, leaving nothing in the handbag!). Needless to say, I listened to my father from then on, and my up till then meagre respect for authority—not to mention my shoulder (ouch!)—began to swell rapidly.

I got through university by hiding in my room (when I wasn't out drinking) and listening to the band Midnight Oil. Despite all my gallivanting around, I graduated in 1984. That's when life really began for me, and that is where the story of this book, taken up in the following chapters, picks up speed.

It is important for me to point out here that at the beginning of my life, I was neither destined for, nor guaranteed, success; nor was I born with a silver spoon in my mouth. In fact, I was a typical troubled youth without a vision, but with plenty of potential. The fact that I have made anything of myself means that anyone reading this book can make something of him or herself. Your fate is not written in the stars. Even if your hand was dealt from the bottom of the deck (which mine was not), you can still make good. There is always hope.

So why did a man with my background write this book about the principles and practices of dreaming up the life you want?

First, let me say that my motivation was to encourage others. I know that if I became successful, anyone can do it. Success belongs to everyone who wants to go after it, everyone who desires it badly enough.

Secondly, I believe that from the vantage point of my life today, with all the benefits and blessings I have, it is time to put something back. I particularly want to help young people, and this is largely due to my wife's influence. Debbie's passion for youth is unquenchable. Like me, Debbie has had many turbulent moments in her own childhood resulting in a tremendous compassion for young people. As you will soon learn in this book, Debbie and I know how hard it is to get a dream for your life or to believe your life could be truly magical. This is especially so when you are a teenager facing all the pressures and challenges of adolescence, in an all-too-confusing world. It is even harder when you have taken a knock or two, when you have experienced rejection or tragedy, or when you have never had anyone, not even your parents, believe in you. A parenting expert I know says that everyone needs at least one person who is irrationally crazy about them; sadly, a lot of young people today don't even have one person to believe in them or to encourage them.

And that leads me to one other reason for writing this book. Of recent times Debbie and I have developed a vision for an Australian organisation called Youth Insearch—which runs camps for youth in need of a fresh start in life, a new dream. It is all about teaching them alternatives.

I have visited the camps YIS runs; they are incredible, designed to put the kids' feet back under them by teaching them at least one necessary life skill—TRUST. That is not an easy lesson to learn if your mum and dad abandoned you at four, if you witnessed your mother or father kill her or himself or, if, as with one young man I know, you have never been hugged, not once in your life.

Part of the proceeds from the sale of this book will go to Youth Insearch, which is an incredible organisation. Their burning passion for Australia's troubled youth is powerful and timely. To quote the YIS website: 'At the camps, a safe and trusting atmosphere is created where young people feel comfortable to discuss emotional issues relating to family breakdown, drug and alcohol abuse, sexual abuse and grief related issues.... Participants are able to draw on the experiences from each other and establish new goals and directions, taking control of their lives and realising their full potential.' We like what YIS stands for—helping kids to help themselves by finding a fresh start, a new dream.

This book is just the start of my link with YIS. Much of my future work, I hope, will contribute to assisting organisations like this one get the vital funds they need to help others find a dream of their own, just as I did. Debbie and I have a vision to be heavily involved with YIS; we believe that vision includes mentoring, equipping and teaching leadership skills to the new and established YIS leaders. If disadvantaged youth have mentors and become accountable to someone they respect, this can have a significant positive impact on their futures. So the vision is for Debbie and I to become a sort of personal mentoring school for YIS kids really longing to change their lives.

Youth Insearch's own story is miraculous, being the brainchild of a man with a heart full of grief. Ron Barr—a living Australian legend—used to visit his drug-addicted son in hospital, a situation that was absolutely crushing him and demoralising his spirit. One day, he had the courage to ask a momentous question: Why are we trying to fix these drug-addicted kids by giving them more drugs? (That was how attempted cures for drug addiction were being affected in Australian hospitals.) As Ron walked sadly back to his car and adjusted his rear view mirror, he said to himself, 'Somebody could change this … somebody could do something …'. Then he caught a glimpse of his own tired and troubled face, and instantly the penny dropped. In that sudden epiphany, his dream—and his life's work — took shape: 'Wait a minute,' he thought, 'I'm somebody!' Ron's wife Judith supported his dream, and the rest is history.

You see, dreams are wonderful yet mysterious things; they powerfully shape what it means to be human. In an emotive scene from the compelling and disturbing film Dead Poets Society, an English teacher, Mr Keating (played by Robin Williams) tries to get Todd Anderson—a quiet introverted boy crushed by the weight of his family's expectations—to find his dream, his calling. Keating compels Todd to stand on his teacher's desk and to call out at the top of his voice these words from American poet, Walt Whitman, 'I sound my barbaric yawp over the rooftops of the world...'. The 'yawp' is the equivalent of a primal cry from the pit of the stomach. It comes from the same place as the dream, and, like the dream, it needs to find a means of escape. By sounding a 'yawp,' and finding a dream, a person leaves their own unique, indelible mark on the world.

At the heart of this inspirational book is a very serious question: What were you created for? What is your destiny, your purpose for living? What were you meant to do with your life? What is the vision that will not only provide you with satisfaction now, but also leave a legacy for your children, grandchildren and friends?

Let's not kid ourselves. Hardly a living soul believes life has no meaning at all. Every person is engaged in the magnificent quest for cosmic significance. Finding a dream is like finding the combination to the safe holding the blueprints to life.

Having a dream means having a vision for your life. A visionary does more than just wake up in the morning, show up at work and come home for an evening meal. A visionary enjoys a life far richer than the person who gets to go fishing once in a while, play golf on weekends and take a three-week holiday at Christmas.

To have a dream is to believe you have a destiny to fulfil and to go after that destiny with every ounce of strength you have, for as long as you have it.

Achieving your dream means obtaining sufficiency of every good thing: a balanced lifestyle; sufficient time for fun and enjoyment of the good things you work for; a stable, happy family life; time to enjoy your children; the deep sense of inner satisfaction that comes from achieving your goals; the attention of others and recognition for what you have accomplished; an abiding sense of purpose.

I once promised myself that the first book I wrote would be called *The Dream is Everything*. Here it is. I write it now with the full force of passion, the benefit of hindsight and the sweetest knowledge of all: that one day I discovered my dream. I recognised what I was meant to do, be and become. I chanced upon my destiny.

This is a book of stories and principles that are taken from my experience as a husband, from conversations I have had, things I have read, or from lessons learned and applied in the context of our business. All of life is an education, but—more than anything and perhaps more than I can express—my marriage to Debbie has been responsible for shaping my perceptions of reality and success. Our relationship has been (and continues to be) the source of much inspiration. Without my life with Debbie, none of the principles you find here would ever have gelled in my head, heart or experience. Debbie was the beginning of—and the inspiration for—all the serious dreaming I have ever done.

This is a book forged on the anvil of trial and error — what you will read are nuggets of precious truth that have been hammered out in the (sometimes painful) process of defining and living our dream.

My story, like so many others, is that of a young man who didn't have a dream. Unlike Winston Churchill or Michael Jordan, whose remarkable stories I refer to more than a few times in this book, I was clueless when it came to what I wanted out of life. I suspect I was on my way to a fate similar to that of the young Florida boy who recently flew his plane into a tall building in a bizarre suicide. To lack a dream is to lack vision, purpose and a sense of destiny. Without a dream there is no reason to live.

Dreams alone explain what we are to make of all the successful people who have climbed mountains, won Olympic Gold medals and sailed round the world, despite mobility challenges, blindness and loss of limbs. If you have the right dream you will be sustained through the many struggles and hardships of life, even your old age and its accompanying trials of physical limitations and failing health.

Living the dream means staying on course until the very end. If you have the right dream, you will do so. To be born—to have a beginning—is to know you will also have an ending. When the power runs down and the dream is fulfilled, it will end. Being a dreamer means knowing that when you do reach the end, you have lived every ounce of your destiny until your body rests of its own accord.

∞   ∞   ∞

In this book I tell the story of what it has meant for Debbie and I to find, pursue and live our dream. What we have learned along the way is here distilled as The Dream is Everything. I believe (I hope not arrogantly) this book to be relevant to businesspeople, students, housewives, professionals, and just about anyone who hungers for a meaningful life. Young people, too, I hope, will be given copies of this book to inspire them, to teach them that life is full of possibility, that there is always hope. Whether you are someone who has been trying to live the dream without success; a young man or woman who has experienced pain and trauma; a budding entrepreneur looking for a vision; or someone who has discovered he or she has been living the wrong dream and is looking for direction—I firmly believe this book is for you.

The book consists of ten short, teaching-oriented chapters. Nowhere do I suggest what your dream should be. (Who would I be to tell you that?) Rather, this work celebrates the uniqueness that every person brings to the adventure called 'life'. What you will find is lots of practical advice related to the core principles and components of what it means to be a dreamer—a visionary.

The themes addressed in this book are all related in some way to envisioning, enlarging and bringing about your dream—having a lifelong vision; destiny; purpose; passion and motivation; having fun; sacrifice; discipline and hard work; integrity and honesty; self-belief and faith in what you cannot see; commitment and stickability; love for self, the dream and others; relationships; the value of community, common cause and association.

I suspect if you read any worthy textbook on sociology, business, marriage, family or ethics, you will see the same themes emerging, for they are basic to what it means to be human. They are also crucial to living 'the dream'.

What is written here on the subject of dreams is by no means exhaustive, and many more examples of dreamers could have been included. What has been written, though, is enough to set you on the pathway to your destiny and to a full experience of humanness in a vibrant, wonderful world.

Peter Cox
Easter 2003

The dream is everything

'TWO ROADS DIVERGED THROUGH A
YELLOW WOOD ...' THUS BEGINS ROBERT
FROST'S IMMORTAL POEM, WHICH ENDS
WITH THE WORDS—'I TOOK THE ONE LESS
TRAVELLED BY/AND THAT HAS MADE ALL
THE DIFFERENCE.'

Isn't it funny how all lives can go in either of two directions: upwards toward the ideal life (the dream) or, sometimes sadly, downwards to intractable poverty, constant failure and purposelessness. Life is full of choices: options. In the case of two roads leading through the woods, we can choose which path we will take: the gentle, untroubled road to nothingness or the off-the-beaten-track rabbit trail to glory, happiness and a life of fulfilled promise.

The choice to go after a meaningful life was never a given for me. It came, quite unexpectedly, out of a realisation one day that things just weren't working. Perhaps as you read this you feel the same way, that something just isn't working—that whatever you were destined for in life isn't emerging as clearly as you thought it would. Take heart. **In a very real sense I turned my life around in a few short hours.**

DECEMBER 11, 1985. 11:00 A.M.
It's been one of those dreadful lovers' fights. I'm wasted. The bright sun is a dot of savage colour in a cloudless sky. It's four days into my vacation on Great Keppel—a resort island in sunny Queensland, Australia. I'm here with my girlfriend of three and a half years.

LIKE A TINY SEED, OUR DREAM GERMINATED THAT DAY

I have no idea where my life is going. I don't know why I am doing anything I do. My relationship with my girlfriend is not where I want it to be.

Suddenly I spot a five-foot-two-inch dark-haired beauty. Olive skin and brown eyes, ... a spirited woman. Something goes off inside me.

Debbie Holden is an aerobics instructor on Great Keppel, and from the moment I lay eyes on her I know I have found something that was missing.

Not something I have lost; something I have never possessed.

Somehow she feels it too. We are on the beach together until the small hours of a still morning, with the bright waters lapping on a golden shore. We talk by moonlight, discovering each other's hopes, exchanging our deepest secrets. The beach is deserted—isolated— we are lost together in a world of our own.

Lying on that beach under the hulking tropical palms, I dream the dream of a lifetime. What I have, what I am today,—just seventeen short years later—I saw it all that night like a mysterious vision: a pleasant house, great kids, money to burn, a butler, cars to die for, fun, friends, freedom, happiness, life in abundance ... . I dream my most honest dream, and for the first time ever I feel completely at ease with myself. If I were to die now, suddenly it seems that it has all been for something.

Like a tiny seed, our dream germinated that day and seventeen years later we are living it. That chance encounter with Debbie Holden changed my life forever. Until then I was going nowhere. My whole life had been about the next cheap thrill—and that had led me down every wrong alleyway imaginable: bad friends, bad deeds and bad debts. **Our story proves it only takes a few**

short hours to change your life for good. (Perhaps even in the time it takes you to read this book.) I felt the echo of our dream rumbling inside me that night, and I knew nothing would ever be the same again. And nothing has been. That night I left everything behind in honest pursuit of the dream. All I had to go on was gut feeling and raw passion. It cost me everything—and gained me everything—to make the decisions I made that night. That's what it means to go after the dream.

> *My girlfriend, the young woman I came to Great Keppel to be with, is sobbing uncontrollably in our hotel room. She knows she has lost me. The next day she leaves me forever, and for the remaining ten glorious days of 'our' vacation, I am with the most captivating woman I will ever meet.*

> DECEMBER 21, 1985.
> *After ten days of surf and fun, I am leaving.*

> *I phone my parents from the island to tell them the 'big' news: I am casting off the yoke of my 'dead-end job' as a marketing assistant and returning to clean pools on Great Keppel. Funnily enough, they don't seem to share my enthusiasm for the grand new vision.*

> *The plane climbs into the sky and I leave the island and a waving Debbie far behind. I'll see her in another ten*

days, but I miss her already. It feels as though the dream is vapourising before it even has a chance to take shape.

I arrive back in Sydney to find at least thirty well-meaning friends and relatives—each one with a piece of advice trawled from the vast depths of their life experiences. Everyone tells me I have done the wrong thing, that I'll regret it. Everyone that is, except one man—my best friend, Craig Bennison. He looks me in the eye and says, 'Mate, something's different about you. Something's happened. This girl has really got to you. Whatever you decide, I support you.'

(YOU ONLY NEED ONE PERSON
WHO BELIEVES IN YOU TO
MAKE THE DREAM A REALITY.)

That night, Craig and I go to a Midnight Oil concert. (The 'Oils' are my favourite band of all time.) I'm at the concert trying to forget about everything. From 20 yards across a crowded hall, with 12,000 people bouncing to the 'Oils', my ex-girlfriend sees me, charges across the room and clocks me with a powder-keg right hand, dropping me to my knees. I go down like a sack. Two bouncers grab us both and lift us off the ground. My ex-girlfriend, like a wounded cat, is throwing everything she's got.

I go home, humiliated, depressed, feeling as low as can be, and confront the terrible emptiness of my life. I turn the key, open the apartment door, turn on the light and the emptiness I feel in my heart becomes palpable. My ex-girlfriend has cleaned out our place. I'm now the proud owner of a dirty old couch and a flea-bitten cat. It's the lowest moment of my very low life.

(THERE'S A PRICE TO HAVING A DREAM.)

For the next ten days I don't eat. My comfort is a bottle of Jim Beam. I drink every night, just so I can sleep. I lose a massive amount of weight.

Ten days later—New Year's Eve. Debbie is due to arrive on a flight from Brisbane.

To help me impress Debbie, my parents went guarantor for me to borrow AUS$10,000 to swap my Datsun 1200 with 200,000 plus miles on the clock for a 'flash' car—a Toyota Celica. I buy it that day in anticipation of Debbie's arrival.

I wait at the airport, clutching a bunch of plastic-wrapped roses. Two hundred passengers disembark the 767 from Brisbane. The last passenger to enter the terminal is dressed head to toe in white—boots, shorts, headband and tank top—the love of my life, Debbie Holden. My heart skips a beat or two; I know we are meant to be together forever. For the next seventeen years I stutter and stall and start again, but the dream that was born in those few hours on the beach at Great Keppel never leaves me. I know I will arrive at the life I have imagined, and I know that somehow Debbie and I will get there together.

∞   ∞   ∞

One year before this, in 1984, with a Bachelor of Business degree under my belt, I had entered the workforce as a marketing assistant for a large Australian company. Each day I banged and bounced my way by bus up Parramatta Road, past the concrete ghetto of used-car dealers and into work. The job was meaningless and dreary, and I brought home a lousy AUS$14,000 per annum. I just couldn't believe this was what I'd grown up to become. I didn't have a dream—I was living a nightmare.

In 1985 Debbie and I met on Great Keppel and one year later, I was still madly in love with Debbie. It wasn't just puppy love or some mad infatuation; this woman set off firecrackers inside me. I wanted Debbie more than life itself.

The trouble was Debbie didn't want me. The euphoria we had both felt on Great Keppel didn't last for Debbie once she got to know the real me.

Debbie was on the rebound from a failed love affair and she had lost all perspective on what love was. However, she was clear on one thing—she did not love me. The knowledge that Debbie didn't love me hurt deeply, but I had to be honest with myself: she saw through me. I was on the road to nowhere. She knew it. I knew it. For all I could tell, the whole world knew it. I had no idea where I was headed in life, no clue as to what my life was about. I had no idea how to translate my Great Keppel vision into reality.

YOU ONLY NEED ONE PERSON WHO BELIEVES IN YOU TO MAKE THE DREAM A REALITY

After throwing in my marketing-assistant role I jumped about from job to job. Nothing ever seemed to fit. I was easily bored. A few weeks before Debbie and I were to get married, I had eleven dollars in the bank. I was about to offer my bride to be my trembling hand (which she didn't really want) and eleven lousy bucks. That was all I had to show for several years of hard sweat in the corporate world. I had no idea how to make our dream work. All I knew was that I didn't want to be stuck in a pointless job on a marginal salary—seen but not heard.

Three weeks before our wedding I went to the beach for a surf, but there were no waves and that left me with plenty of time to think. Time to think about how lost I was, and how messed up I had to be to be marrying a woman who didn't love me.

While I was on the beach that day, our lives changed in a very powerful way. Debbie met a very talented former work colleague who showed her a business we could get into. Debbie caught the vision and knew it was the right plan for us. She dreamed a big dream; a dream that took root in her heart and began to grow.

Three weeks later we walked down the aisle—very much out of love (at least, on Debbie's side). I had a great pain in my heart because this wonderful woman I was crazy about didn't love me.

TRANSLATE THAT ... VISION INTO REALITY

By now I was working as a marketing manager for a large tobacco conglomerate. I was responsible for managing our marketing efforts at the Australian Formula One Grand Prix and I had to break the awful news to Debbie that because of my work commitments, I couldn't go on our honeymoon to Bali.

Working the Grand Prix circuit I was rubbing shoulders with a new class of people. Shaking hands with drivers like Nelson Piquet and Johnny Herbert, I felt the confidence oozing out of them. There was something in their eyes, and they had that 'I-can-do-it' aura that goes with winning. I wanted what they had, but I still lacked a way to make the dream real.

By February the following year, Debbie had press-ganged me into attending a promotional conference to find out more about the business opportunity she was so keen on. I had been dragging my heels, but as I listened to the success stories of people who had gotten into the business and become hugely successful, I kept thinking, 'I could do this! Why not me?'

That night was the kick-start I needed. I had a vision on the beach at Great Keppel, but I needed a vehicle to get there. I needed help to get going. The business Debbie was shown gave us a way forward.

My first goal was pretty material in nature—I just wanted to own a Porsche 911, which cost a couple of hundred thousand dollars and was way out of my league—but the dream took root. We set up our home-based business, got out there, made our cold-calls, showed our marketing plan, and started to grow our business.

It has been fourteen fruitful years since that motivational conference—sixteen and a half since the birth of the original dream on Great Keppel. Debbie and I (now very much in love) run a multi-million-dollar business, with product distribution in many countries around the globe. Today, we live a life most people would not relate to: we own a beautiful home in a fashionable suburb; we have enough money to send our two children to the best schools; and we can afford the sort of holidays most people can only dream about. We manage our own time and run a global business giving us every possible satisfaction.

We got here from nowhere because of the dream. I was on the wrong path through the woods until I discovered that dream. When I found the dream it was easy to recognise the right road. We have achieved and enjoyed more dreams than we can count, and our dreams just keep getting bigger and better.

What is a dream? How do I get one? How do I achieve my dream? *This book has been written to help you answer these questions.*

We got here
from
nowhere
because of
the dream

GET A DREAM THAT
MOTIVATES TODAY'S EFFORTS

Do you have a single dream for your life—something you would like to be, do or become? If you don't, I urge you to get a dream.

You may be reading this in the midst of corporate bedlam, writing computer programs for IBM or filing tax returns for small business people. You may be climbing the corporate ladder, rung by clawing rung. Perhaps you are a busy CEO making it all happen. But what's your dream? What do you want your life to be like? Are you happy today with where things are? Are you on the right road?

What you do today should be motivated by your dream. Any work you do should open doors to the fulfilment of the dream. Whatever you pour your life's blood, sweat and tears into, must be motivated by your dream. But if you have no dream, how can you know you are spending your energy and talents on the best things? A wise man once said: 'What you will be in the future you are becoming today.' If you don't have a dream that motivates all you do today, you must get one.

On November 15, 1899, during the Boer War, a young English journalist found himself on a train with British soldiers. A large company of Boers (Nationalist Dutch and German farmers from the Orange Free State in South Africa) ambushed the train between Colenso and Ladysmith in the Natal province. With stones laid on the train track, the train, reversing, shuddered to a crashing halt. Several cars spilled sideways onto the grassy veldt in a smoking ruin. When the leading British officer was injured, the young journalist took command, saving many lives through his heroism, daring and courage under fire. After guiding many to safety, he returned to the scene of the train wreck and was captured.

Shipped north to Pretoria and confined, he escaped within weeks, fled to the coast and took a tramp steamer back to

Durban. Two weeks later he gave his first political speech on the steps of the Durban Town Hall. Somewhere in that adventure the young journalist found a dream—a dream of who he could become, what his life could stand for. That dream was later fulfilled when the young journalist went on to become the great wartime Prime Minister of Britain, Winston Churchill.

I repeat: what you do today must always be motivated by a long-haul dream. Winston Churchill grasped his present opportunity because he had a long-term dream.

WANT TO BE AVERAGE? JUST WAKE UP ...

There are many pearls of wisdom in the children's story *Alice in Wonderland*. One is particularly relevant to our discussion. When Alice comes to a fork in the road, she asks the Cheshire cat which road she should take.

'Where do you want to go?' he asked her.

'I don't know,' she replied.

'Then it doesn't much matter which road you choose,' he told her.

If you want to be average, just wake up in the morning. To be above average requires more than just being awake; you need a dream. A dream gives you direction. A dream makes sure your passions are not misdirected.

If you don't know where you are going, how do you know which road to choose?

KNOW YOUR DREAM

Every person dreams a different dream from his or her neighbour. There are as many visions of life as there are people, but there are defining qualities common to all dreams. For instance, your dream will always put fire in your belly, and get you excited—you won't need to stoke the fires of motivation.

Whatever your dream is, you must know it so well that you can taste it, touch it and feel it.

YOUR DREAM IS EMOTIONAL ENERGY

Your dream is pure, raw, emotional energy. It should burst out of you like steam from a pressure valve. Getting a dream means being unafraid to get emotional: to go to those places where your true feelings and gut urges hide. Too many people are afraid of their feelings and they end up living a tragic lie.

The dream is pure truth, because it is the real you. Strip away lies, subterfuge, expectations and hysterical hype—what are you really left with? What makes you tick? If you could have the ideal life—what would it look like? When you can write your vision down, you are beginning to be clearer about the dream. You are beginning to taste it and feel it.

Here are the rules for getting your dream started:

- let your emotions run wild
- don't squash your passion
- have the guts to go for your biggest dream
- put yourself in a place where it hurts to go.

When Debbie and I started dreaming, we got emotional about it. Our dream to run our own business and be 'time rich' was so powerful that we could almost touch it. We wanted it so badly, we cried sometimes. We fostered that passion and let it burn powerfully in us.

OTHERS WON'T APPRECIATE YOUR DREAMS

Mick Jagger, one of the most successful rock musicians ever, came from a middle-class London family. Can you imagine how Mick's father felt when young Mick brought home a nice, clean-cut(!) boy like Keith Richards, and boldly pronounced, 'Mum, Dad, I'm dropping out of school, and Keith and I are starting a band called *The Rolling Stones*'? It's fair to say that, back in the 1960s, Mr and Mrs Jagger may not have seen the full benefits of allowing Mick to follow his dream. Since then, however, the Stones have become one of the most successful rock bands of all time, delighting millions of fans worldwide, and earning obscene amounts of money. In 2002 he even received a knighthood for 'services to popular music'.

Four decades ago, nobody could have foreseen just how successful Mick and the boys would become. Nobody, that is, except Mick and the Stones. Which is fair enough. After all, it was their dream.

I am not suggesting for a minute that Mick and the boys should be held up as role models to follow in all aspects of their lives—but they are role models for the dream. *They believed of themselves what nobody else believed possible, and they succeeded.* Dreamers know how to touch, taste and feel every vision they ever have— long before they can actually see it or handle it.

YOUR DREAM IS YOUR HOPE

No one can live for long without hope. As a wise friend once quoted to me: 'If one truly had lost hope, he would not be on hand to say so ...'. Your dream is a constant source of hope.

Victor Frankl, the Austrian psychologist survived the Auschwitz death camp. He lived to ask himself the fundamental question: Why did I survive when others died? And the question that followed that one: Why did so many survivors of the death camps commit suicide on their release? Having struggled for so long to live in the face of the inhuman conditions and brutal treatment of a concentration camp, why did these wretched souls, once freed, no longer want to live?

YOUR DREAM IS A CONSTANT SOURCE OF HOPE

The answer Frankl found was hope. He desperately wanted to survive Auschwitz and to see his family again. Frankl had a dream that he could taste, touch and feel. Frankl's dream stoked a fire in his belly. And Frankl, as opposed to others, lived. Frankl also kept hoping for the future—and that is what stoked his passion to live long after the events of the holocaust.

Hope keeps you alive. Hope gives you the strength to go via the road less travelled.

A FEW FINAL THOUGHTS

- LIFE WITHOUT A DREAM IS NO LIFE AT ALL.
- WANT TO BE AVERAGE? JUST WAKE UP ...
- DREAMERS KNOW HOW TO TOUCH, TASTE AND FEEL THEIR HOPES.
- LIFE WITHOUT A DREAM IS A TOTAL WASTE OF AN OTHERWISE VALUABLE OPPORTUNITY.
- HAVING A DREAM WON'T BE EASY—NOBODY WILL LOVE YOU MORE BECAUSE YOU SEE WHAT THEY DON'T.

Fire in the belly

A *year or two ago I flew from Frankfurt, where I
had been on business, to Singapore. Standing in
the maelstrom that is Changi—Asia's busiest
airport—I spotted a distinguished looking lady of
about 60 years. What struck me about her was her
dignity and poise; she seemed unaffected by the
chaos about her. She had a quiet confidence; she
seemed to know who she was, and yet she carried
herself with quiet humility.*

*I noticed the stunning jewellery draping her elegant
and slender wrists; amazing diamond rings flashed on
her manicured hands. I was so struck by the charm of
this woman and her amazing jewels that I approached
and struck up a conversation.*

*'Excuse me,' I said, genuinely interested in this
marvellous lady, 'but I couldn't help noticing that ring
on your hand; it is amazing, and I know my wife
would love it. Would you mind if I asked about it?'*

The lady's eyes sparkled like fresh-cut gems; she could see I truly appreciated the splendour of the gold and precious stones on her fingers.

'Why, yes,' she trilled charmingly, and proceeded to tell me all about the rings. I ended up sitting next to this lady and her husband. She graciously asked me about myself, so I explained my business, its global opportunities and some of my future aspirations. 'What you've got to understand,' I said with conviction, 'is that I'm a dreamer.'

THE RIGHT
DREAM
DROPS
PASSION IN
YOUR GUT

The woman then explained that she and her husband were running one of Australia's largest wholesale food and liquor marketing companies. 'You won't believe it,' I said, 'but I had my first job in the marketing department of your firm.'

At that, her husband's head perked up, and we quickly chatted about my life in his firm. I couldn't believe I was sitting next to two of Australia's wealthiest entrepreneurs, so I took my chance to listen, learn and soak up some wisdom.

At one point I asked them, 'Did you always know your business would grow so big?'

'Oh, goodness, no,' the lady laughed. 'We just built the business because we loved our family and wanted to do something for them. We've even employed some of our kids. We never knew how big it would become, but we just took every opportunity to follow our dream. Sometimes we had the chance to buy a private airplane or some other luxury but we bought another warehouse instead; we sunk the money back into the business.' She concluded, 'We had fire in our bellies and we just let our dream grow and expand.'

Then she turned to me and asked, 'Peter, do you still remember making your first million?'

'I sure do,' I said, with more than a little pride.

'I still remember making our first billion,' she responded gracefully. I felt totally humbled.

'Fire in the belly': that phrase has stuck with me over the years. At the time it got me thinking. Why did Debbie and I succeed? How did we grow our business to a multi-million-dollar global operation? How did our stormy relationship turn into such a loving

marriage? How did we hang together when so many other troubled marriages like ours went the way of the divorce courts? Now I had an answer: we had fire in our bellies. *We wanted our dream so badly, we were willing to do anything to fulfill it.*

FIRE IN THE BELLY ... YOU'VE FOUND THE RIGHT DREAM

The right dream drops passion in your gut. If the dream isn't putting fire in your belly, you've got the wrong dream. The dream will inevitably generate passion, because a life vision always comes complete with its own internal motivation.

Find a quiet space alone and sit down where you can't be interrupted. Ask yourself what you are passionate about; what gets you excited; what gets you out of bed in the morning. Find the fire in the belly, and you've found your dream.

When you get your dream crystal clear in your mind, you will have fire in your belly. That fire will be aroused quite naturally because your dream will be an extension of who you truly are. You won't be living a lie pretending you want certain things out of life when you really desire others. Your life will start to have a ring of integrity about it.

In the first book of J.R.R. Tolkien's trilogy, *The Lord of the Rings*, the fellowship of nine, including Frodo Baggins, the pocket-sized hero whose fate is wrapped up with the Dark Lord Sauron's ring, sits in the vast darkness of the Mines of Moria. In that fearful place, the wizard Gandalf tells Frodo that Sauron's ring did not come to him by chance; that possessing it is his destiny—'It was meant to come to you, Frodo ...'.

YOUR DREAM IS WHAT YOU WERE MADE FOR

I believe each of us, like Frodo Baggins, is created with a purpose—something we were meant to do and destined to become. That is the dream. It's not always about money, possessions or power—it is about finding out what you want, what you were made for, and going after those things.

It is my belief that we were all created for some higher purpose: **each one of us was born to achieve something specific.** That's the dream. Your purpose will be your contribution to the world and it will be unique to you. Like so many Frodo Bagginses in a world of 'big' people, each one of us is an unlikely hero. Very little separates heroic winners from cowardly losers—nothing more than a dream and fire in the belly.

Growing our business, making money and acquiring material things were never really what the dream was about for Debbie and me. (Okay, I admit, the Porsche 911 got me going, but that was never the whole story. The material benefits are merely byproducts of the dream.) *Our business was merely the vehicle for fulfilling our dream*. We had fire in our bellies to succeed in business not because we might get rich, but because it would bring about our dream to be free to be 'time rich'.

NOTHING IS ACHIEVED
WITHOUT FIRE IN THE BELLY

YOUR PURPOSE WILL BE YOUR CONTRIBUTION TO THE WORLD AND IT WILL BE UNIQUE TO YOU

Whatever your dream is, you will know it when you find it, because you discover a fire in your belly. You will experience a great knot of passion when you think about the dream.

Michael Jordan—one of the greatest sportspersons of the last century—is a hero of mine, and an exceptional example of the dream putting fire in your belly. Jordan has won countless playoff MVP awards in the NBA (America's national basketball competition), six championship rings (three each between 1991-1993 and 1996-1998), and two Olympic gold medals. He has achieved every notable honour awarded in his field of sport, including the record for the most career scoring titles (ten—including seven in consecutive years).

In 1994, Jordan came out with a book, the title of which sums up his philosophy on life—I Can't Accept Not Trying: Michael

Jordon on the Pursuit of Excellence. That's what fire in the belly gives you—a determination to win.

Motivated by the dream to play professional basketball, Jordan was discouraged early on when he was dishearteningly cut from the basketball squad in high school. But fire in the belly gave Jordan the edge. Jordan chose to ignore family and friends who advised him to pursue a secure future by enlisting with the US navy. Instead, he went to North Carolina University (NCU) to pursue his basketball dream. He worked harder than ever in the off-season to force his way back into the squad. The rest is history. He was the first freshman to ever play college basketball for NCU.

> *I realized that if I was going to achieve*
> *anything in life I had to be aggressive.*
> *I had to get out there and go for it.*
> *I don't believe you can achieve anything*
> *by being passive. I know fear is an obstacle for*
> *some people but it's an illusion for me.*
> MICHAEL JORDAN,
> professional basketballer

Winston Churchill's dream may once have been no bigger than to give a rousing speech on the steps of the Durban Town Hall. But with the advent of World War II, Churchill's dream had to grow—and Churchill had to grow along with it.

Fire in the belly motivated some of the most powerful oratory ever heard from this man. His dream of a victorious Britain gave Churchill the conviction to inspire his hurting people and the raw courage to declare: 'We shall never surrender' when London was a smoking pile of rubble, blitzed day and night by the most potent air force in Europe—the German Luftwaffe.

Take any worthwhile dream—from winning a war to becoming the world's best in a sporting endeavour—it will be fire in the belly that gets the job done. And don't assume such passion will be well received. Anyone who dreams will experience rejection and insult; that's all the more reason to find the right dream—the dream that gives you the fire in the belly necessary to fight for your dream against great odds.

OTHER PEOPLE WILL REJECT YOUR PASSION

If I had a dollar for every time I was told I would fail, I'd be as wealthy as the two entrepreneurs I met on my recent plane journey. But the negative energy in such throwaway comments merely fuelled my dream: I soaked up that corrosive acid and let it fuel me. Every negative put-down, each knock-back and every criticism helped me make another call, show my sales plan and keep my business growing.

You must do the same with your dream. Some people will never believe in your dream; they'll even rejoice at opportunities to put down your passion. **But it doesn't matter whether others believe in your dream; it only matters that you believe in it.**

> *When my son Dane was born in 1994 something went off inside me, and I knew I had to get a lot more serious about the dream. Parents find fire in their bellies because they want to give their kids a great life, even better than they had, and to leave them with a great legacy. In this way our kids help us find the dream, and give us the motivation to succeed.*

> *Between 1989 and 1992, when I was working in the corporate world as well as trying to build our business, Debbie's and my relationship was the source of much pain. We lived like two strangers, and when we did see each other, there was anger, resentment and constant bickering. It was a nightmare. But I managed to turn that pain inward and let it put fire in my belly.*

> *In retrospect, it was foolish to think that to work things out with Debbie I had to build our business to the point where I could quit my job and semi-retire. My belief that this would give us the time to work on loving each other and save our marriage was probably naïve. But at the time it was what kept me going. Debbie was part of my dream, a part I wasn't willing to live without. I had fire in the belly about saving my*

marriage. As I left our little rented house in Sans Souci every day on my way to work, I would look back at the darkened windows and the pitch-black emptiness. I was lonely beyond telling, but I continued to dream the dream. I kept fuelling myself with a mental image of Debbie in love with me, and a couple of kids—their contented laughter ringing in my ears—waving me off as I drove out the driveway to build our business.

... IT ONLY MATTERS THAT YOU BELIEVE IN IT

That was all a dream. I couldn't see it. I couldn't even imagine how it would come true. But I believed it. I had faith. I clung to that dream, and that dream gave me the passion to push myself harder and to do the things that the other guys wouldn't do. That's how fire in the belly helps you fulfil your dreams. That's how we succeeded.

For Debbie to finally love me took some hard work on my part. I had to become the sort of man she needed me to be, and that took some doing. Suffice it to say, that only fire in the belly kept Debbie coming home to me, and only fire in the belly helped me become the man she could love and respect. It took a lot of hard work and commitment—from both of us—but that is what the dream inspires in you.

I'm not recommending marital pain as a means to build your dream: I'd be the first to tell you to get your house in order so you don't have to operate out of that awful, lonely place. But what I am saying is that fire in the belly gets you to your dream. You have to use every means possible—even negative energy—to fuel your efforts if you truly want your dream to come true.

Without fire in the belly, your dream is impossible—it is nothing more than wishful thinking.

A FEW FINAL THOUGHTS

- DEVELOP A PASSION AND IDENTIFY YOUR DREAM.
- WHEN YOU FEEL TRULY PASSIONATE ABOUT SOMETHING THEN YOU ARE IN DREAM TERRITORY.
- THE DREAM ALWAYS COMES WITH ITS OWN MOTIVATION.
- YOUR DREAM IS UNIQUE TO YOU AND WILL FIT YOU LIKE A GLOVE.
- THE REALLY BIG DREAMS REQUIRE FIRE IN THE BELLY.
- REJECTION IS PART AND PARCEL OF DREAMING.
- DON'T WORRY IF OTHERS REJECT YOUR PASSION— THAT, TOO, COMES WITH THE TERRITORY.
- IT DOESN'T MATTER IF OTHERS BELIEVE IN YOUR DREAM, IT ONLY MATTERS THAT YOU BELIEVE IN IT.

Have some fun

The year is 1999—the place: Rimini, Italy. Thousands of screaming dreamers cram into a large auditorium. The air is thick with sweat and emotions are running high. A Canadian rocker arrives on stage to the twang of electric guitars, the throb of drums and the crowd goes wild. The screams are deafening.

Gyrating to a backing tape, the singer grabs the mike. As the lights come up so does the noise level, and the crowd is gripped by the sight of their superstar in the flesh. There is a surge of people toward the stage: a tidal wave of human bodies. The wave shudders and falls back as the rocker begins to belt out some powerful, rock rhythms.

The crowd sways under the rocker's magnetic power. Hands clap, feet drift and passion is aroused. But this is not your average rock audience in the throws of drug and alcohol induced hysteria. This is a business conference for dreamers. This is no ordinary Canadian rocker. This is Peter Cox making yet another dream come true.

Many people mistakenly believe the road to their dreams must be dreary, like a bad novel or a movie lacking a plot. They think the dream is all about hard work. But if the dream is all cost and no payback in terms of simple pleasure, then you've got the wrong dream.

Life has got to be fun. The journey toward your dream should be enjoyable, or else why bother trying to fulfil it?

> **fun** n. & adj. —n. 1 amusement, esp.especially lively or playful **2** a source of this **3** exciting or amusing goings-on —adj. amusing, entertaining, enjoyable (a fun thing to do)
> THE CONCISE OXFORD DICTIONARY (10TH ED.)

In making your dream come true, you must make room for fun, enjoyment and pleasure. This is non-negotiable for genuine success.

When I leap about the stage having taken on the persona of a famous rock musician, I do something incredibly basic: I enjoy myself. When I enjoy myself I send a clear signal to all whom I influence: the dream is not only about making money, growing a huge organisation or gaining power. On the contrary, the dream is also about fun, pleasure and enjoyment.

Since I was a little boy I have nurtured a dream of being a rock musician, despite the fact that I have never had a single singing lesson. Over the years I have studied and practiced the movements, mannerisms and voices of many of my favourite rock musicians to the point where I now delight in impersonating some of my rock idols before an audience of thousands.

The Nightriders (my 'band') consists entirely of people in my business circle, even though they can hardly play a chord between them. The show is a total fake. We put plastic pads on the drums so we don't make too much noise, and we squelch the backing tape. We are having a ball in a make-believe world.

We rehearse at midnight in a dusty and decrepit recording studio in Sydney. Half the time we take the studio over from a real-life band of musical hopefuls who have dropped buckets of sweat on the concrete floor just so they can pull off some forgettable pub gig the following Friday. Meanwhile, the Nightriders play to audiences of up to 8,000 screaming dreamers.

We all chuckle when we see our names on the schedule posted on the studio door:

9.00-11.00 p.m.'The Dead Accountants'
11.00 p.m.-12.00 a.m. 'The Nightriders'

When the guys in the other bands hear the polished sounds emerging from the studio they probably think, 'Gee—those guys are hot!' Little do they know the 'tight' sound has nothing whatsoever to do with the Nightriders, and everything to do with a backing tape.

I believe we add real value to every business training conference I speak at because our performances offer living proof that the dream, though deadly serious, always leaves room for playfulness and enjoyment.

IT'S THE WRONG DREAM IF YOU'RE NOT ENJOYING THE JOURNEY

Too many people go through life without enjoying it. **But you don't have the right dream if you don't enjoy the journey.** You will work hard to get to your dream; reaching your goal should be a delight. Your dream should make you a bigger, better human not a shrunken killjoy fulminating against the joie de vivre of others. No matter what you do while executing the dream, make sure you enjoy it.

It's easy to talk about fun, but for some people enjoying life just doesn't come naturally. Some people even consider fun and hard work to be incompatible. I am reminded of the story of the little boy whose mother shouted down the stairs, 'Johnny, hurry or you'll miss school.' Little Johnny replied: 'Mum, I may be late, but believe me, I won't miss it.' For many of us, childhood experiences (including our education) have conspired to teach us that life is not supposed to be fun. Rubbish! Where does it actually say that? I know work must be disciplined, serious and focused, but does that mean you can't enjoy it too?

One question I am often asked is: How do you cultivate fun in your life when you are so earnest about dreaming and bringing those visions to reality? My answer is, in part, that I follow this simple recipe:

- I hang around with people who make me laugh.
- I exercise constantly because I believe fun is impossible if you are not physically fit.
- I reward myself with things I enjoy when I achieve a key goal.
- I spend lots of time with my wife and children.
- I create magic moments for others.

DREAMS WORTH HAVING USUALLY REQUIRE MORE THAN JUST YOUR EFFORTS

Within my organisation I do everything possible to engender spontaneous fun, both for staff and associates. I hire a limousine once in a while and entertain key people over dinner. I take a corporate box at the Rugby League, and 'shout' everyone a night on the town. My dream is fun for me, and I want it to be fun for my team, too.

Academic studies of successful, growing companies consistently prove that a fun team environment gets better results (in terms of goals achieved, rates of sick leave and absenteeism and bottom-line profitability) than does a dreary, overly stringent environment. Dreams worth having usually require more than just your efforts. Teamwork is what accomplishes the big tasks. And the team that plays together, says the old chestnut, stays together.

No matter what your chosen career or business, you must find ways to create fun for everyone, including yourself and your family. If you are not having fun at work, this will spill over negatively into your family time. I do not suggest that you start your own band—anyway, I don't want nor need the competition (!)—but there must be dozens of things you would enjoy doing if you would only take the time to think about it.

THE DREAM IS UNCOMFORTABLE, THAT'S HALF THE FUN

Although the dream is fun, it is not always comfortable. Do you think I always feel comfortable taking on the persona of a rock muso? Do you think I have not more than once broken into a cold sweat before climbing into my gear and strutting onto a stage in front of thousands of people, knowing I could make a real goose of myself? That's the whole point—your dream should take you to places where you aren't comfortable. That is half the fun.

When I first dragged the guys into the Nightriders, they were pretty uncomfortable, but I wanted them to learn this life-shaping lesson: your dream can make you uncomfortable—and if it doesn't do so, then it's probably far too small. For you, the dream may not include rock stardom, but it will still take you to places you may not naturally want to go. Unfortunately, too many of us are put off the right track by our fear of discomfort.

TAKE EVERY CHANCE TO LAUGH...IT MAY SAVE YOUR LIFE

The famous comedian, Groucho Marx, is reputed to have said: 'A clown is like an aspirin, only he works twice as fast.' Medical studies show that people who laugh a lot have better overall health and less heart disease and cancer than people who don't. Laughter, like physical exertion, releases good chemicals—known as endorphins—into the blood stream. Endorphins are recognised as one of the human body's self-healing mechanisms. If you're not laughing and having fun, you may literally be killing yourself or allowing yourself to die earlier than you need to. Cancer and heart disease are the two biggest killers in the developed world. Remember, you've got to be alive to enjoy the dream and the dream should include a long life in as good a health as possible.

Under situations of stress the human body produces a natural hormone called epinephrine. Epinephrine can do untold damage to the finely tuned workings of your body, and that is why stress

---

[3] C.Sowell.'Is Laughter the best medicine?'Quest, vol.3:4 (Fall, 1996)

is so dangerous. It is also why we need to laugh a lot, because laughter suppresses epinephrine. Laughter also increases the production of T-cells and other immune-system cells that attack viruses and diseases. Further, it raises and lowers your heart rate, giving you a cardio-vascular workout. And laying aside all these benefits, don't you just enjoy a good belly laugh?

Laughter will keep you enjoying your dream longer, and being a joker may save your life—now that's something they never taught you at school. So, why not be the guy in your team or business who surprises everyone with a daily laugh? You may be surprised at the results.

... YOU MUST FIND WAYS TO CREATE FUN FOR EVERYONE

Having fun also means leaving room for good, honest jocularity—even at your own expense.

Debbie and I love to go to the public auctions in Leichhardt, Sydney. I enjoy the buzz of bidding for items of interest. On one particular evening Debbie had disappeared and I was bidding amidst a huge crowd. I had targeted a painting that caught my eye, and I figured it could not go for more than a few hundred bucks.

I started bidding, but I was shocked at how quickly we passed the $200 mark; the price just kept escalating. Up it went to stratospheric levels. Before I knew it, it was on its way into orbit. Who was bidding? I looked around but couldn't see anyone.

Finally, out of the corner of my eye I caught sight of just who was bidding up the price—it had now gone way, way, way above my expectations. There was Debbie with a huge grin on her pretty face. We laughed and laughed about that. You just have to find ways to laugh, even at yourself.

> *It is the chiefest point of happiness that a man is*
> *willing to be what he is ...*
> DESIDERIUS ERASMUS (1466-1536),
> *a Renaissance scholar*

A FEW FINAL THOUGHTS

- NO MATTER HOW HARD YOU WORK FOR YOUR DREAM ... YOU'RE STILL ALLOWED TO HAVE FUN.
- THE HARDER YOU WORK FOR YOUR DREAM, THE MORE ROOM FOR FUN YOU MUST ALLOW YOURSELF.
- LAUGH OFTEN; LAUGH ALL THE TIME ... CREATE POSITIVE ENERGY.
- FUN DREAMS ARE OFTEN UNCOMFORTABLE, BUT PINS AND NEEDLES ARE FUNNY TOO.
- SUCCESSFUL PEOPLE NEED A MINIMUM DAILY ALLOWANCE OF SEINFELD.

Pay the price

An Australian record blue marlin was caught on January 16, 1998, 28 nautical miles north east of Bateman's Bay in a boat 5.75 metres in length.

A 37-kg line was used and the catch took three hours. There was no gaff on board so a rope had to be tied through the marlin's mouth and out its gills to secure it (which resulted in many layers of skin being torn from a man's arm due to the rasp-like nature of a marlin's throat). Due to its immense size, the marlin was towed behind the boat—it weighed 417.6 kg and measured 4.6 metres in length. Part of the proud angler's prize was a fibreglass cast of the blue marlin that he now has mounted on a wall in his home.

That satisfied angler was Mr David Leighton, the father of one of my closest friends and business partners. To this day the marlin hangs in pride of place in David's garage den.

Recently, one of my friends who is a keen fisherman, let me in on the secrets of big game fishing. While the opportunity to get out on the water among the brotherhood of boaties is an attraction in itself, it is the chance to catch 'the big one', to pit his skills against a wonderful sea creature much heavier than he is, and to bring that big fish up to the boat, that really gets my friend excited.

...ATTAINING
YOUR DREAM
CAN COST
YOU
EVERYTHING
AND MORE

Half the fun with big game fishing is using light tackle. Light tackle is purpose built to make it more difficult—more sporting—to land the big one. Let's face it, a big game fish has the power to break even the heaviest line and tackle, so when you bring one in on light tackle it makes the victory all the sweeter.

But there's a price to pay. Light tackle makes it harder work for you, the angler. You have to play the fish, using up its strength as your own fails, hour after gruelling, sweat-soaked hour. A fight with a big marlin or shark can last six hours or more. The fish starts out stronger than you, but it's who finishes the stronger that counts.

In the end, it is not strength and brute force that will bring that trophy fish to the boat—it is hard work, endurance and commitment to the fight. After a strike, you batten down the hatches and hold on for the ride of your life. For the first little while, the fish will do anything it can to spit the hook, and in many cases a game fish succeeds—that's part of the fun of the contest.

After a few hours, however, things settle down and it becomes a war of attrition, with neither side asking or giving quarter. One fact is certain: as much as you want to catch the fish, it does not want to be caught. After a few hours of hauling, in which the fish has run too many times to remember, your back is stiff and aching and every sinew in your body screams at you to back off and throw in the towel. But you can't: the adrenalin is running and you're as hooked as the fish on your line—maybe more so.

At the end, win or lose, you know you have been in a battle. That fish will not come to the boat willingly, and unless you are 100% committed to the contest—unless you give it every ounce of strength, courage and passion you can muster—you can forget about landing that fish. One thing my friend has learned about big game fish: they are 100% committed to escaping, and only 100% dedication on your part will bring them in. **Without giving all you have and more—crossing pain** thresholds you didn't know existed—you can kiss your fish goodbye.

The same is true of the dream...

Never, never, never give up ...
WINSTON CHURCHILL
wartime Prime Minister of Great Britain

Aristotle, the great Greek philosopher and orator, in the fourth century BC had everyone who would ever live figured out. He wrote a book called Art of Rhetoric (public-speaking) and in it he laid out the psychological profile of the human being. What he wrote over 2300 years ago is as true today as it was when the paint on the Athenian Parthenon was still fresh. Aristotle argued that there are two basic motivations behind all human behaviour: seeking pleasure and avoiding pain.

WELCOME TO SUCCESS...THE PRICE IS PAIN

Until now we have focused on the pleasurable aspects of pursuing the dream. However, the road to your destiny often comes at a tremendous price: attaining your dream can cost you everything and more.

Because success is inevitably linked with pain, and because it is human nature to avoid pain, the majority of human beings are more attuned to avoiding success than to achieving it. We love success and we wish to attain our dreams, but few of us are willing to pay the price to make our dreams a reality.

Don't fall into pain-avoidance mode

It is difficult, if not impossible, for the average person in the pain-avoidance mode to dream a big dream. The bigger the dream, the bigger the price-tag. The smaller the dream the less cost and the less pain.

But consider the cost, if only in terms of missed opportunity, of not achieving the dream. Pain-avoidance is not a rational calculation; it is emotional and spiritual cowardice. You are not being noble when you fail to dream, you are being carnal—operating at the level of the butterflies in your belly. We are body, soul and spirit, and the best—higher—parts of us can dream, believe, and even calculate that pain today might be a worthy price to pay to purchase the fullest human experience. Will you let your fear of rejection or failure rob you of your vision of the good life?

If no human being had had the guts to run the gauntlet of nagging doubt, personal discomfort and brutal pain, there would never have been any military victories, marathon gold medals, mountains climbed or babies born. We must not live at the level of pain avoidance. To be fully alive, we must find a dream and be willing to pay the price to achieve it.

DON'T ACCEPT OR MAKE EXCUSES FOR MEDIOCRITY

It may sound harsh but given everything we now know about human nature, we should be afraid whenever we catch ourselves making excuses. The biggest temptation we face is to justify our lack of application to the principle of paying the price.

It is the nature of human beings to justify their own mediocrity. Mediocrity: the word comes from the Latin and its literal meaning is 'half way up a stony hill'. Thus, mediocrity is, 'a halfway house for quitters',—those who got half way and gave up—no doubt justifying their decision all the way down the mountain and all the way home. **The decisions of mediocre people are formed in the gut in a context of fear and pain avoidance,** but are justified in the head as eminently rational and reasonable approaches to life.

When you catch yourself making excuses or justifying mediocrity in yourself, you must ask yourself, 'Do I really want to attain this goal or dream? If I do, what price am I willing to pay?'

Heather Turland is a hero of mine. She is a diminutive, marathon-running mother of four who is determined to be the best marathon runner in the world. As a mother of four children it wasn't easy for her to keep up such a gruelling schedule, but she pounded out hundreds of kilometres every month in preparation for the 1998 Commonwealth Games. She knows what it is to pay the price—to go through pain barriers no one else wants to go through. She is realistic about the pain, and she doesn't like it. In the opening lines to her autobiography, *Gold Beyond Your Dreams*, she writes:[4]

The pain paid off when she went home with a gold medal.

> '*I hate running 10 kilometres. Ten kilometres is too short because it's a burst. It's short, it's fast and it hurts. I don't really like running anything shorter than a 21-km half-marathon.*'

> *It's easy to spot a successful person—*
> *They do the things unsuccessful people don't do …*

> *Success is not a matter of avoiding things—*
> *It's a matter of doing other things …*

Heather Turland knows what success costs. She could easily have rationalised or justified non-participation. If the pain had got too great she could have walked away with her head held high. But she didn't baulk at the pain: she took it into account and continued to actively pursue her dream. And she won gold.

SACRIFICE … THE KEY TO SUCCESS IN LIFE

[4]Turland, H & Lowell, T (1998). *Gold beyond your dream: The Heather Turland story of winning life's marathon.* Melbourne: Information Australia. p. xiii.

Most people don't want to succeed because it costs too much. 'I'm okay, mate ...' 'She'll be right, mate ...'—these are the words of the average person who just wakes up in the morning. Success is not an issue for them, because they never dream a single dream. If the dream does make its presence felt, it's usually too frightening for them, and they try to block it out of their minds. The problem is that these people are usually miserable in their mediocrity.

If you are not happy with where you are in life, and if your dreams aren't coming true, then you must pay the price to get off your current treadmill. To get where you want to go in life will take sacrifice. Sacrifice means paying the price; setting the dream apart as the 'pearl of great price' and being prepared to dedicate yourself wholeheartedly to it. Sacrifice demands singular devotion—a decision to stick to one successful course of action, no matter the cost.

There is a simple test used to calculate emotional intelligence (EQ), which is widely regarded as the best predictor (better than IQ) of success in life. The jellybean test is easy to apply: you put a few kids in a room, offer them a jellybean each and say, 'I'm leaving the room now. If you don't eat this jellybean while I'm gone, I'll give you five jellybeans when I come back.'

The math is easy to work out, the kids are better off waiting: in the same way delaying gratification is the key to emotional intelligence. Perhaps surprisingly, the kids who eat the one jellybean, despite the five on offer, are in the majority—they're the people who are just getting up in the morning. Very few people—only the dreamers—will pass up an instant reward for a greater potential reward.

TO PAY THE PRICE IT HAS TO BE THE RIGHT DREAM

Nobody ever paid the price for success who did not understand that price as integral to their dream. You won't pay the price unless the dream is truly yours—unless you own it.

Australian mountaineer Brigitte Muir is an inspirational dreamer who has climbed the world's highest summits, i.e. the highest peak on seven continents. The introduction to her autobiography, *Wind in My Hair*, describes how she found her dream:

> *It was at the foot of Victoria's majestic Mount*
> *Arapiles that Brigitte Muir first conceived the dream*
> *to climb the highest mountain on each continent ... .*
> *It was a dream she saved up for nine years, and a*
> *dream that endured illness, hardship and heartache.*[5]

Brigitte Muir is a superstar of mountain climbing, and she had to pay a huge price for her dream—personally, physically

---

[5]Muir, B. (1998). *Wind in My Hair.* Ringwood, VIC: Viking

and emotionally. But if the dream puts fire in your belly and you are having fun fulfilling your dream, you'll want to pay the price.

Jack Nicklaus, one of the greatest golfers ever, is reported to have hit over 10 million balls on the practice tee over his career. Ten million balls! That's paying the price. It is no surprise, then, that Nicklaus had the lowest scoring average in professional golf eight times, and was the highest PGA money winner eight times. Nicklaus won 18 majors over his career—more (so far) than the great Tiger Woods, and 16 more than Australian champion golfer Greg Norman.

Nicklaus' experience shows us that certain aspects of success can be boring. But don't let the boredom fool you. Hitting 10 million golf balls may be boring, but it wins tournaments and fulfils dreams. **The difference between winners and losers is not that winners have paid the price and losers haven't. It's that winners have paid the *bigger* price**—a price that includes such things as the boredom of repetition, loneliness and hardship.

When I first started to grow my business internationally, flying the thousands of miles I flew was a killer. It was lonely. Leaving my wife, leaving my kids—I could hardly stand to do it. Seeing Dane wrapped around my legs trying to prevent me from getting in the car, and Debbie sobbing her heart out knowing I was headed off to some place we had never heard of so I could grow our business—that was pain. But in all that travel lay the seeds of our serious success and the ultimate fulfilment of the dream. That's what success takes.

During those difficult times you must be absolutely clear why you are paying the price and you must truly believe the dream is worth achieving; that it is your dream. When things get really bad, when you are five hours into the fight with the marlin, you will question yourself, 'Why am I doing this? Will this be worth it? Do I really want this? Can I really pay the price?'

That is why, before you get to that place, you must be clear about your dream, your aims, your willingness to pay the highest price, and your readiness to go through the kind of pain that the average human being avoids. That's what paying the price is all about.

A FEW FINAL THOUGHTS

- NOBODY WHO ACHIEVED ANYTHING GREAT, DID SO WITHOUT PAYING A PRICE.
- THE PRICE OF YOUR SUCCESS IS PAIN.
- PAIN AVOIDANCE IS YOUR WORST ENEMY.
- NEVER COUNTENANCE YOUR OWN FLIMSY EXCUSES.
- THE BIGGER YOUR DREAM, THE BIGGER THE PRICE.
- SACRIFICE IS YOUR BEST FRIEND.
- NO PAIN...NO DREAM.

Discipline

*A*t 7:00 a.m. (3-4 days a week) —rain, hail or shine—I jump in the car and head down to a little hotel near my house where there's a gym. Not a flash gym, mind you. The equipment's a little run down and the machines aren't as new as they could be. The lights are dim and there's nobody there to see what goes on.

It's often cold and uninviting. In fact, frequently I would rather not go. But I'm 40 years old. My dream is to be a young 40. It's not vanity: I just want to look my best and be my best. I figure a little effort won't hurt, but at 6:00 a.m. on a cold winter morning, when I think about getting up, it hurts.

A lot of days I'd much rather stay in bed, pull the blankets over my head and just sleep in. Then I think of my two boys—they see everything I do. They will imitate what I do and set themselves up for life by following the patterns I have set for them. **So it's** important that they see Dad being disciplined about his goals.

The beauty of showing up regularly at the gym, no matter how I feel, is the payoff of feeling good about myself—knowing that I have been disciplined about my goals and that the significant others in my life, like my kids, have benefited from my discipline.

DISCIPLINE: DOING IT WHEN YOU DON'T WANT TO DO IT

Discipline means, apart from anything else, having routines: doing the same things all the time. Not the things that unsuccessful people do, but the things unsuccessful people won't do. That also means doing things when you don't want to do them.

My routines often drive Debbie crazy, but at least I have them. I wasn't always like this. I'm a sanguine personality and I love people. I am not, by nature, a disciplined person, though I do love hard work. But in building our business I soon realised that without discipline, achieving the dream was just wishful thinking. As a result, I have taught myself to be disciplined.

I once asked a top Australian fund manager—responsible for billions of dollars worth of equity funds—what his work habits were for a typical day. He told me that every night he prepares his desk by clearing it. Then he compiles a list, in order of priority, of his top ten tasks for the following morning. He makes sure to list at the top his hardest work—the work he least wants to do—and he always completes those tasks before moving on to the tasks he enjoys doing. Now, that's discipline.

In any work, in any attempt to bring a dream to reality, there will be odious chores. Discipline helps you complete these tasks, as does the motivating knowledge that they are crucial to achieving your dream. You may fear cold calling. You may detest sales presentations. The voice of discipline will tell you to do them consistently and with passion; by so doing you will succeed.

SUCCESS MEANS DEVELOPING DAILY HABITS

When someone asks me what are the keys to success—how I fulfil the dream—I respond with a question of my own, 'What are your daily habits? I don't care what your dream is; what are you doing to achieve it?' Unless a person is ready to answer that question, all other discussion is a waste of time. When I look at people's daily habits, I am usually able to ascertain what their dreams are and whether or not they will go on to achieve them.

Ian Thorpe, champion Australian swimmer, has a dream to win Olympic Gold. Such a dream is commendable, even laudable. The fact that Ian goes to the pool every day tells you he is serious about the dream. The fact that he daily swims disciplined kilometres tells you he is a champion: **a champion is someone with the discipline and the daily habits necessary to attain his or her dreams.**

When I hit 36, I thought I had arrived. There was enough money coming in from the business that Debbie and I no longer needed to work—other than to keep team motivation and team building on the agenda. I got to a point where I was getting out of bed at 8:30 a.m., and sometimes as late as 10:00 a.m. I knew I lacked discipline, and I also knew that to grow my business globally in the face of competition, I'd have to get tougher and push myself further. I had a dream to go international with what we were doing. I had fire in the belly about where that would take us, and I knew it would be fun to go there. However, I also knew I would have to pay the price, and that kept leading me back to one conclusion—I needed discipline.

I knew I didn't have the discipline, so I decided to get it. For me, that meant

... DO THEM
CONSISTENTLY
AND WITH
PASSION;
BY SO
DOING
YOU WILL
SUCCEED

paying a fitness trainer. My fitness trainer, Dave, gave me accountability. On a cold, dark, rainy morning, when I didn't feel like going to the gym, I knew Dave would be there—and I knew I had to show up, no matter how I felt.

DAILY HABITS DEVELOP ACCOUNTABILITY

One of the best sources of motivation for accountability is your family. Your husband or wife and children are an enormous part of your dream. Finding a partner to love for a lifetime and raising children together can provide you with the type of accountability you need in order to be disciplined.

Winners want to be held accountable, and they love to get structured accountability in place. International motivator, Pat Mesiti, has this to say in his book, *Dreamers Never Sleep*:

Sacrifice. Discipline. Commitment. Perseverance. Faithfulness. Loyalty. Delayed gratification. Feeling nauseous yet? These words conjure up mental images of pain, agony and years of frustration in search of a dream. They're becoming less and less popular, especially to the Leisure-Pleasure Generation of today.[5]

---

[5]Mesiti, P.(1998). *Dreamers never sleep.* Castle Hill, NSW: Pat Mesiti Ministries. p. 131.

If it's that hard to develop discipline, how will any of us do it? Only by being kept accountable! If we say we will do something, we must do it. Accountability keeps us moving toward our goals.

There are many talented sportspeople who will never be champions. Not because they lack ability. They just don't have the disciplined routines necessary to successfully execute their dreams. The same is true of many talented business people: some are writing talent cheques their disciplines never let them cash.

BEING ABOVE AVERAGE MEANS HAVING AN 'AVERAGE' DAY

If you want to succeed and fulfil your dreams, the key is very simple: get disciplined about success.

I have a plan by which I attack each day—every day.

6:00 a.m.	Get up
7:00 a.m.	Go to the gym (3-4 days)
8:30 a.m.	Take my kids to school
9:00 a.m.	Breakfast
10:00 a.m. - 1:00 p.m.	Work in the office
1:00 - 3:00 p.m.	Sport/quality time with Debbie
3:00 - 5:00 p.m.	Quality time with the kids
5:00 - 6:00 p.m.	Work in the office
6:00 p.m.	Dinner/family time
7:30 p.m	Put the kids to bed and grab some time with Debbie

8:00 p.m.	Flexible—time for Debbie and I, time alone or with friends
12:00 a.m.	Bed

This is my average day. I am not saying it will be right for you. Copying my day would be fruitless if it didn't suit your schedule or dream. The key is to recognise you need a disciplined schedule in which you fulfil the tasks necessary to accomplish your dream.

> *Short-term and long-term plans are the key to self-organisation. Write them out so they can be regularly reviewed, revised and followed.*
> DR ANTONY KIDMAN,
> *father of actress, Nicole Kidman*[7]

Having clearly defined plans and the discipline to follow them is a non-negotiable for champions. So is the commitment to follow through on these plans even when the going gets tough. That's why putting your plans in writing can be so strategic. I believe once you have 'published' something—on paper or verbally—you have made yourself more accountable.

Discipline leads to clear thinking, and enhances execution of the dream. You have time to think, plan and clarify progress. The

---

[7]Kidman, A.(1998). *From thought to action.* Sydney: BGS.

vast gulf between well-disciplined and ill-disciplined people is not measured in dollars but in mess. Disciplined people do not mire themselves under a mountain of paperwork. Dreamers rarely find themselves looking for documents they urgently need under a growing weight of yet-to-be-dealt-with communication. Instead, they get organised.

Disciplined people are as near to being on top of just about everything as they can be. This is because they let their well-designed plans (not their emotions) dictate the activities they undertake. They do not spend their time putting out brushfires, because they don't camp in tinder-dry forests.

DISCIPLINE MEANS PLANNING

Every year, I write a personal and business plan. I take my dream and break it down into annual targets—precise goals that I need to achieve. Then, whenever I fly somewhere, I take my plan along as reading material. In this way I try to get the plan into my head so it will control all my actions for the coming year. I also send a copy of it to my personal mentor, Jim Dornan, for review and invite his feedback and criticism.

I believe you need an updated plan for your life every year—a plan that details your personal goals, as well as those for your business, and your family. Planning takes discipline; it takes effort; it takes sitting down and thinking. **Success doesn't just happen—it takes hard work.**

In 1991 General Norman Schwarzkopf was appointed Commander-in-chief of the American forces during the Gulf War. Every night, subsequent to that, he would lay a copy of the Bible—open to the book of Joshua—on his bedside table. He disciplined himself to read the Old Testament book over and over and to think about it until he had developed a battle plan—a strategy that would win the war against Iraq and save as many lives as possible. That's planning—it takes discipline and hardheaded grunt.

Once I have my plan (including specific goals for that year), I ask myself the question, 'How will I achieve my plan?' The answer to that question gives me my yearly strategy. My strategy (macro) then needs to be broken down into specific tactics (micro). For example, Winston Churchill's strategy in World War II was to fight off the German air force, get the Americans to enter the war, and retake Europe. In terms of specific tactics, he made sure the British air force was as ready as it could be; he kept up the morale of the English people; and he built air raid shelters. These were specific tactics applied within a larger strategy.

In writing my annual plan, I am committing myself to accountability. Once I have put myself out on a limb and said I will do or achieve certain things, the significant others in my life—my wife, family, friends and business colleagues—can hold me accountable. Accountability increases my motivation and ultimately my power to accomplish the dream, thus making my plan more than wishful thinking.

Congratulations, you've arrived—
But it's going to take you 20 years to build
anything great!
JIM DORNAN,
after Debbie and I reached our first major business milestone

The dream is a marathon. It may take many years to achieve. You must plan for success. Discipline, year in, year out, will be the key to making the dream a reality.

A FEW FINAL THOUGHTS

- REMEMBER, DISCIPLINED PEOPLE DO THE THINGS THAT UNSUCCESSFUL PEOPLE DON'T DO.
- DISCIPLINE IS DOING IT WHEN YOU DON'T WANT TO.
- SUCCESSFUL PEOPLE LIVE BY HABIT.
- SUCCESSFUL PEOPLE HAVE MORE 'AVERAGE DAYS' THAN AVERAGE PEOPLE DO.
- PLANNING IS NEVER, EVER A WASTE OF TIME.
- PRACTICE MAKES PERFECT, SO BE DISCIPLINED ABOUT PRACTICE.

Keep your integrity intact

Jim Dornan is a global entrepreneur and a personal mentor to myself and Debbie. Jim has dreamed bigger dreams than I could ever imagine. Today he runs an organisation touching hundreds of thousands of people in more countries than I can count. But that—as impressive as it is—isn't what really impresses me about Jim Dornan or makes me receptive to his leadership and mentoring.

There's something else that makes me admire Jim and makes me want to emulate him—his integrity. **To Jim, the dream is so precious, that he refuses to let any lapse of character spoil his chance of achieving it.** He is committed to being a man of his word and he always follows through, without fail. Jim never compromises on ethics, not even for an instant.

Jim once casually recounted an incident during a trip to the Caribbean where he had purchased a valuable piece of jewellery. Although he could have worn the jewellery when passing through customs and claimed it as a personal possession, Jim declared its purchase, paid the duty on it and kept his conscience clean. That story says it all. I don't know about you but I may have been tempted—just a little—to wear the jewellery, keep my eyes down, and walk on through. But that's not integrity, is it? Integrity is putting a higher price on your reputation than any sum you can name.

Something else Jim once said has stuck with me. I had asked him what was the key to success in business. His answer tells you everything about the man: 'Make the right decisions for the right reasons—not for convenience … .'

Integrity is one of those really 'big' life words. It has to do with wholeness, integration, being unbroken. When it comes to the dream, you and I must place such a huge value on integrity that we won't allow anything to undermine it.

The dream is the real you—the you that emerges when all other opinions and traditions are stripped away. If the dream corrupts you or causes you to do things you don't want to do—things that may be convenient but dishonest, or that make life easier while altering your core principles—then you have the wrong dream. In my view, the dream will never shrink you; it will only enlarge you.

There is a sad story that underscores how easily people with a dream can be corrupted. Lee Strobel, an award-winning investigative journalist with the Chicago Tribune, and a Master's Graduate of Yale Law School, couldn't believe his luck when he stumbled on a cache of secret Ford Motor Company documents in the late 1970s. Strobel, on checking the court file in Winamac, Indiana (USA), uncovered shocking evidence of what key executives at Ford had known for some time: the Ford Pinto automobile was a fire danger when hit from behind at around 20 miles per hour. The documents also proved that Ford executives decided against improving the car's safety specifications to save a few dollars per vehicle and to improve luggage space.

As a consequence of Strobel's findings, Ford was prosecuted for reckless homicide in the fiery death of three teenagers in a subcompact Pinto. So can the biggest dreamers fall without a strong sense of ethics.

> *You're not a man till you can look me*
> *in the eye and tell me the truth ...*
> FATHER OF ACTOR, *George Clooney*

Darren Beadman was the most successful Australian jockey of his generation. In Daylight Ahead: The Darren Beadman Story, he describes a crisis in his own life when he was accused of illegal riding in the mid 1990s. He goes on to record how on his return to racing (having failed to clear his name despite his protestations of innocence) he went on to win the Melbourne Cup (one of the three richest horse-races in the world) for the second time.

In the book Beadman points out that what got him all the great rides, in the top races, was his integrity. People trusted him despite his brush with the racing authorities. That was because back in the years when Beadman was an apprentice jockey, Beadman had stayed true to himself despite attempts by dishonest men to corrupt him. It was that integrity, more than fine horsemanship, he believed, that got him onto the best horses, into the greatest races, and managed by the elite trainers—and from there, first across the line.

INTEGRITY MEANS BEING UNWILLING TO DICE WITH THE DREAM ...

That's a gutsy admission when you think about it. Beadman readily admits he won not necessarily because he was the best jockey, but because he stayed true to his calling and kept his integrity intact. He knows he would never have been in the big races in winning positions had he not kept the dream pure.

Our dreams can never be fulfilled in their purest, sweetest or most desirable forms if we are prepared to sacrifice them for a few trinkets or baubles along the way. Integrity means being unwilling to dice with the dream or play fast and loose. **Integrity opens the door to dream-fulfilment in ways we cannot even imagine.**

In life it is so easy to forget that who you are behind closed doors is who you really are. The real key to achieving the dream is not who I am in my public persona but who I am when no one's around. The private me is the real me. Question: 'Who are you when no one else is looking?'

INTEGRITY MEANS KEEPING YOUR WORD

Many business people and leaders sadly believe that it is a case of what they say goes, no matter how they themselves behave. But words and actions, like two parallel lines, should always run together. The great Israelite King and ex-shepherd, David, wrote: 'Happy is the man who gives his word—even if it hurts to keep it ... .' That's my highly inaccurate paraphrase, but it captures the idea. It's easy to make a promise, but hang around in the trenches of business or management long enough and promises have a way of getting broken.

David was a skillful shepherd from a small town—Bethlehem—who went on to run a huge kingdom out of Iron-Age Jerusalem. Despite the fact that he made some huge mistakes—like we all do—David was a man of his word. That's why other people trusted him.

Giving your word means making promises, and promises are an integral part of business and relationships. Sadly, breaking such promises appears to have become commonplace. We must understand that we rob ourselves of power in every area of life if we break our promises. When it comes to the dream, let nothing sully it: say what you mean and mean what you say!

Cheat someone once, or wrong them, and you may lose their friendship, loyalty and respect forever. The key words in this sentence are 'once' and 'forever'. One small slip can bring down the whole shooting match. A lack of integrity has the same power as the mythical kryptonite: it will steal every ounce of (moral) strength you possess. Trust, once eroded, is not easily regained.

INTEGRITY IS LOYALTY ... DESPITE OTHER OFFERS

In life we are constantly faced with offers—job offers, relationship offers and even, sadly, drug offers. And I don't just mean crack or heroin. Anything that lures you away from following your dream is a narcotic—a short-term fix. If your dream is so big you can taste it, you won't spoil it with a cheap detour down narcotics lane.

The dream only comes to fruition if you stay the course, never wavering from your core convictions. Loyalty is a non-negotiable—loyalty to your vision, your family, your faith, your boss or mentor and the people with whom or for whom you work.

Will you get other offers on the road to your dream? Sure. There are detours and enticing billboards on every major highway headed for the dream. The key is to look out for the road signs, and recognise a detour when you see it—a road that goes nowhere near where your dream is taking you.

In the recently released film *The Patriot*, actor Mel Gibson plays Colonel Benjamin Martin of the US Continental army. After the ruthless murder of two of his sons, Colonel Martin is tempted to abandon his war against the British. His grief threatens to derail him from his pursuit of the ultimate dream—a free America, self-governed and without interference from the British Crown. The message Martin's friends give him is vital, 'Stay the course,' they tell him, 'don't jump ship before the dream is fully realised.'

GOOD CHARACTER BUILDS TRUST AND TRUST IS THE GLUE OF RELATIONSHIPS

Anybody can achieve short-term success but to be great over a long period—to achieve the really big dreams—requires unalloyed devotion to your peers, team and family.

In the 1980s, when Microsoft was developing the Windows™ operating system, the designers, led by Bill Gates, spent 18 months living, eating and sleeping Windows™ in their offices in Seattle. Twenty-four-hour days were the norm in the battle to get their operating system first to the market. What kept that team together and enabled them to achieve that truly impressive dream? Loyalty, conviction and passion for one another! People had to trust that while they were losing their personal freedom and family time because of Windows™, so were all their peers. In other words, they needed to know everyone on the team was paying the same price and showing the same level of commitment to one another.

LOYALTY MEANS YOU ARE COMMITTED
TO OTHERS – NO MATTER WHAT

British General John Monash (1865-1931) once said:
> *'I don't care a damn for your loyal service when*
> *you think I am right; when I really want it most is when*
> *you think I am wrong.'*

Being a person of substance and a person of integrity demands that you be unmoved in your steadfast support of others' dreams. Even when you see how badly they have messed up. The dream is far bigger than any one mistake; so cut everyone some slack! That is what big people do for one another. Integrity means not giving up on those around you just because they let you down. Commit yourself to relationships in any sphere the dream may take you.

CHARACTER BUILDS TRUST

There are many practical reasons to develop, and be a person of, good character. Good character builds trust and trust is the glue of relationship. Like it or not, relationships are the cornerstone of all serious business dealings. People need to know there's a trustworthy human being on the other end of the phone line or handshake— someone who won't run at the first sign of trouble, someone who isn't only in the relationship for a fast buck. People want to believe they won't be hurt, let down, ripped off, or disappointed.

Building the big dream means displaying consistent and predictable character day in day out, in public and in private. That way people will always know you can be trusted and are dependable.

BECOME A PERSON OF SUBSTANCE

To become a person of influence—a leader, a dream fulfiller— you must first become a person of substance. A substance is something you can touch, taste, feel or smell; it is something real and firm. In the same way, a person of substance has a depth and realness about him or her. Whenever there's a question about what a person of substance may have done or not done, said or not said, asked for or not asked for, people can fall back upon what they know of the person's character. 'Hey, that doesn't sound great, but I know so-and-so, he wouldn't be in that ... I'd better check this out with him ... .' Having that sort of reputation—substance—in people's minds may save you from many problems that have their source in rumour.

WHEN ALL IS SAID AND DONE, THE BIGGEST MISTAKE YOU CAN MAKE IS TO DEVIATE FROM THE PATHWAY OF HONESTY AND TRANSPARENCY

Being a person with substance will also mean you are less likely to overreact when your peers challenge you. People with substance can handle being questioned because they know there'll be only the appearance of smoke, but no fire. They do not mind being asked—and even challenged—about their attitudes or behaviour, because they have nothing to hide. By contrast, when you an 'artful dodger' with things to hide, too much of your energy goes into scheming and covering up. Time spent covering over potential scandals may mean your dream is never reached or you may be forced to be satisfied with a shallow version of the dream.

Of course, when you are a substance-less person there tends to be a lot of smoke around, for the good reason that there is a fire out there. Take the Clinton presidency as an example (1993-2001). Bill Clinton was an Arkansas lawyer and a Rhodes scholar at Oxford University who went on to achieve the extraordinary feat of rolling an incumbent president who had just won a war. In his role as President of the USA he was, essentially, CEO of one of the largest nation on earth. The budgets and expense accounts were huge. Clinton had everything going for him—charm, wit, good looks, oratory skills—but many people believe he lacked substance. (Now, to be fair, Clinton may have been unlucky—he may in fact be an example of perception not being reality. I am not really in a position to know either way.)

So what went wrong with the fairy tale? The Clinton presidency (at least as far as we can see from the outside) was hijacked by lurid scandals, constant accusations of indecency and lingering rumours of business malfeasance. For most of his presidency he was under investigation for some scam or dodgy deal (all of which, to be fair, he credited to his enemies).

Whether Clinton was guilty of anything or not is beside the point, let's be clear about something: a lack of substance on your or my part will bite us every time. Even when we get to our dream—as Clinton did—it will never be as good as it could have been. So make a commitment to invest in your integrity, and to be a person of substance!

When all is said and done, the biggest mistake you or I can make is to deviate from the pathway of honesty and transparency.

A FEW FINAL THOUGHTS

- EVERY DECISION IMPACTS YOUR LIFE—SO CHOOSE CAREFULLY.
- INTEGRITY MEANS KEEPING YOUR WORD.
- ONCE YOU LOSE INTEGRITY, THE DREAM IS SO MUCH HARDER TO ACHIEVE.
- DREAMERS ARE ALWAYS LOYAL.
- CHARACTER-BASED LEADERSHIP IS ALL ABOUT BUILDING TRUST.
- BE TRANSPARENT—RUMOURS ALWAYS DO MORE HARM THAN THE TRUTH.
- PUBLICLY OWN YOUR MISTAKES ... AND SAY SORRY.
- INTEGRITY FEEDS ON A STEADY DIET OF HUMBLE PIE.
- TRUE FRIENDS STICK AROUND TO SEE THE DREAM BECOME A REALITY.
- YOUR REPUTATION IS ALL YOU TAKE TO THE GRAVE.
- YOUR NAME OPENS YOUR NEXT DOOR.
- THE BIGGER YOUR NAME THE BIGGER YOUR NEXT FALL.

Faith

In 1991, the Australian Grand Prix took take place in Adelaide. Two outstanding and skillful drivers represented the Benetton team: Nigel Mansel, an experienced driver from the UK, and Michael Schumacher, a young German who was just cutting his teeth in Formula One racing.

The conditions were wet for the pre-racing for pole position. Schumacher and Mansel had gone head to head on an extremely slick surface but Mansel had prevailed and, with a faster set of lap times, was placed ahead of Schumacher on the grid.

I stood at the back of the room at the after-trial press conference. Cameras clicked, flashbulbs blinked, and journalists fired questions one after the other at the two drivers who seemed ill at ease with each other.

When a journalist asked about the rivalry between the two Benetton teammates, Mansel turned to Schumacher and said firmly, 'Michael, you have what it takes to become a great driver, but you're taking big risks, and if you don't slow down you may not be around for very long.'

The very next day I stood in the pit lane close to the action. It was pouring with rain. The checkered flag dropped. Mansel and Ayrton Senna went bumper to bumper at the front. Schumacher took off from behind, flew down the side of the track, inches off a brick guard wall, and swung out in front of Mansel, blasting past him in one furious movement. In an instant he was gone.

I stared wide-eyed in the pit lane, my heart in my mouth. I couldn't believe what I had just witnessed. I am still thunderstruck by the speed and precision of Schumacher's driving that day.

I am mad about Formula One racing. The sheer speed at which a top F1 driver is handling his vehicle leaves me with goose bumps an inch high. To be a great F1 driver is to possess enormous faith in oneself, as well as in others.

When we talk about the need for faith in pursuing the dream, I can think of no greater example than Michael Schumacher. To date he has more than 50 race wins from over 160 starts, with four individual driver's championships (and one more on the way). Think about it: inserting yourself into a car capable of 340 kmph speeds requires huge self-belief. One small mistake in an F1 race could be fatal. Schumacher does it week in, week out— he stares death in the eye on a daily basis and defies it.

In F1 racing you not only need to be a great driver, you have to possess nerves of steel and lightning reflexes. You have to believe not only in yourself and your own abilities, but you also have to place your faith in the guys screwing on the wheels and in your competitors. Any mistakes and the consequences could affect many lives.

Why is Schumacher such a magnificent champion? Why is he virtually unbeatable under all conditions? Do the other guys on the track not have the faith to push their Ferraris, McLarens or Jaguars to their ultimate limits? Schumacher evidently does. Schumacher has a dream and the faith to believe he can achieve it.

The dream is all about faith—'seeing' what doesn't yet exist. When you find your dream, you may not see how it could possibly ever become a reality. When the dream first emerges, it doesn't usually come with an action plan, a set of instructions, or a how-to manual. You may have to live with the tension of not immediately finding the way to fulfill your dreams.

My initial dream was to have enough time to play golf and to own a Porsche and for Debbie and me to be happy together, and hopefully, one day, blessed with children. But in the early days of our marriage, sitting at home, desperately lonely, never really knowing where Debbie was, I couldn't see how my dream would ever become a reality. At the time it was just wishful thinking. And yet today it is my reality.

Don't be fooled into thinking you can only believe in what you can physically see: that is the worst form of materialism. Half the time what you can only visualise in your mind's eye is more real than what your optic nerves can trace.

The problem with dreaming is that you get a powerful vision for what you want. Fire in your belly stokes your desires. You want your dream so bad you're willing to do anything, go through any trial and pay any price. But then fear sets in ... where do you begin? How long will it take? Where will you draw the strength and patience? Doubt begins to gnaw away at you. And very quickly your dream seems so fragile and delicate that even a small puff of wind might blow it away.

WHEN THE DREAM BEGINS, FAITH IS ALL YOU POSSESS.

That's the way all dreams start. Climbing mountains, winning wars, walking on the moon, starting technology companies and listing on the share market, surviving Auschwitz—these are all dreams that start out so fragile that those who dream them wonder how on earth they'll ever come about. At this point, you have two choices: consigning your dream to the annals of 'great but unworkable ideas' or allowing it to become a living testament to 'faith in what you can't see'.

Just remember that for human society to have come as far as it has, people had to dream dreams of things they couldn't actually see happening. **A dream is by definition an unreality—a figment of your imagination.** What turns unreality into reality is the faith you have that it can be real, and a commitment to working through the process of turning your dream into reality. When the dream begins, faith is all you actually possess.

Jeff Bezos, CEO of Internet E-bookseller Amazon.com is a remarkable man. Certainly, the US NASDAQ share-price index has had its ups and downs over the last few years, and investors are no longer pumping small fortunes into companies like Amazon; nevertheless, Bezos' place in history is secure as a gutsy dreamer who saw what others didn't see. Indeed, in 1999, influential Time magazine voted him its Person of the Year. Here's what *Time* said about Bezos:

> *It's easy to sit here today [1999] nodding about the power of electrified commerce. But back in the day when you—frankly, when everyone—was poohpoohing the idea of online sales, there were a few people who believed. One of them, on a summer day in 1994, quit his lucrative job at a New York City investment firm, packed up and, with his wife driving, made a now legendary voyage to Seattle to start what he thought would be a good business. By the time he arrived there he had a plan to sell books over the*

Internet. Investors thought he was crazy ...

... Every time a seismic shift takes place in our economy, there are people who feel the vibrations long before the rest of us do, vibrations so strong they demand action—action that can seem rash, even stupid. Ferry owner Cornelius Vanderbilt jumped ship when he saw the railroads coming. Thomas Watson Jr, overwhelmed by his sense that computers would be everywhere even when they were nowhere, bet his father's office-machine company on it: IBM.[8]

That places Bezos in some pretty distinguished company. But the key to keep in mind is: Bezos was in it when few saw it. He is a dreamer, a visionary and whether he fails or succeeds with Amazon.com, he has faith to burn.

When Debbie and I started our business our home life was a wreck. That three and a half years later—despite marital tumult and our complete lack of togetherness—we walked out onto a stage before thousands of people to celebrate reaching our first big dream in business, is nothing short of a major miracle and one of the great hope-inspiring features of our story together. **That we achieved such success despite deep personal confusion is unquestionable testimony to the greatness and power of the**

---

[8]Amazingperson.com: Time Magazine Person of the Year(1999). www.time.com/time/poy

dream—a dream that appeared at first sight to be so vaporous that had we whispered, it would have disappeared.

> *We grow great by dreams. All big men are dreamers.*
> *They see things in the soft haze of a spring day or in*
> *the red fire of a long winter's evening. Some of us let*
> *these great dreams die, but others nourish and*
> *protect them, nurse them through bad days till they*
> *bring them to the sunshine and the light which come*
> *always to those who sincerely hope that their dreams*
> *will come true.*
> WOODROW WILSON, *former US President*

'Faith,' says one of the biblical writers, 'is the substance of things hoped for'. The only thing tangible about the dream is the hope you carry like a torch in your heart that it can become a reality. That's right—only hope. What you hope for is all that exists at the beginning. When you're out there dreaming big dreams and everyone else says you've lost it, all you can hang onto is your hope.

Success Magazine, an American publication 'for today's entrepreneurial mind' each year honours renegades—those who defy convention, and triumph over the naysayers. Here's what *Success* wrote several years ago:

> *Some would consider renegades unreasonable people*
> *because they reject conventional thinking and the*

*narrow vision of others. ... Without the acts of
creativity committed by the unreasonable few, we'd
still be painting pictures on cave walls.*

*... There would be no progress without the
unreasonable efforts of men and women. It is
renegades that make a country great, by pushing past
what others think are reasonable approaches, to
create unthought—of opportunities. Renegades
operate in the realm of the unknown.*[9]

Renegades live in hope—not for what is seen but for what is
unseen. They have faith. They are dreamers. We, too, need this
faith when the dreams we visualise are still 'unrealities'; we need
this faith because the dream can seem incredibly unreasonable;
and because all big dreams meet with powerful opposition
designed to derail us.

FAITH...BECAUSE THE DREAM IS AN 'UNREALITY'

The dream is the opposite of reality—it is unreality. In the
beginning, it is nothing but a vision.

The first real step of faith we ever took in our lives—was to set
up our business. We couldn't see it. It was just a vision—a

---

[9] Cited in, Buttrose, I. (1997). *A word to the wise*. Sydney: KEG

complete 'unreality', a figment of our imagination. Like most business start-ups, there was literally nothing in existence.

No stock. No sales force (except for Debbie and myself). No customers. People mocked us, because nobody else could see our dream. What they could see very clearly, was its complete unreality. Our dream was a fiction.

The great irony is that the smaller your dream, the easier it is for both you and others to see it. The flip side, of course, is that when your dream is enormous, nobody can see it.

Taking your panel-beating shop from $500,000 to $10,000,000 in turnover might be too huge a dream for you to visualise a pathway, but the fact that you can't see how you will achieve it is irrelevant. If it's the right dream, it can be done.

In the first decade after 1900, sitting in a patent office in Zurich, Switzerland, a young and, up until then, largely unheralded science teacher called Albert Einstein had a revelation. He hit upon a formula that related matter to energy—up until then in physics the two systems (matter and energy) had been treated as separate disciplines. In a stroke of genius, and one simple formula ($E = MC2$) Einstein pulled them both together.

The formula $E = MC2$ tells us that matter (M) is actually only energy (E) in a different state, and that the principle of unlocking the energy in matter (M) is related to the speed of light (C2).[10] The principle inherent in the formula was a revelation that has since led to the development of everything from simple neon signs to nuclear warheads. The key point for our reflection is this: Einstein *knew* the formula to be true for many years before it was ever conclusively proved. *Einstein believed without actually being able to prove the formula or to see it.*

FAITH…BECAUSE THE DREAM IS SO OFTEN UNREASONABLE

Because dreams are an unreality, they often appear unreasonable. The bigger your dream, the greater the cost and the longer it will take to achieve. The longer a dream takes to realise, the harder it will be to keep going in the face of knock-backs, refusals, opposition and hardship. Faith is the only thing that keeps the dream alive at these times—the raw conviction that what you can't see can still become a reality.

The unreasonableness of Debbie's and my dream was obvious as we struggled in the first four or five markets we entered. When we first opened up in Eastern Europe, for example, there were only costs—no payback. All we could 'see' was money haemorrhaging from our business and our cash flow being bled dry. Thousands and thousands of dollars were disappearing on

[10]The letter C stands for the Latin *celeritas*, meaning 'speed'. As such, the formula (E=MC2) refers to the speed of light squared, multiplied by mass or matter – that's how much enery inheres in a particle of matter.

airfares, hotels, phone calls and the like. Faith alone kept us going.

Today, however, our Eastern European business is highly successful and has paid us back fully for any investment we made—not to mention the wonderful relationships and friendships we enjoy as a byproduct of our business affairs. When it comes to the dream, not 'seeing' something is no criterion by which to judge its reality.

When US industrial automaker Henry Ford began in the 1920s and 1930s to break the work of his assembly lines down into smaller and smaller components and to specialise his workforce to each of these tasks, people thought he was mad. But he only saw what others didn't see. Not long after industrial production underwent a massive revolution that saw Ford's idea become standard practice. Likewise, when the rolling assembly line was introduced into car plants, critics said it was laughable and impractical. Today it is standard industry practice.

Don't be put off by how unreasonable your dream may seem. The seeds of its greatness may very well be inherent in its profound unreasonableness.

FAITH...BECAUSE THE DREAM COMES WITH BUILT-IN OPPOSITION

Dreams are often unreasonable and fly in the face of conventional wisdom. Every visionary encounters his or her share of opposition. Any dream worth dreaming will attract its share of conflict. It may come from your shareholders, a partner, or trusted colleague. Perhaps someone on your team won't agree with your tactics. But if there's no opposition to what you're doing, you're not working the dream muscles hard enough.

DON'T BE PUT OFF BY HOW UNREASONABLE YOUR DREAM MAY BE

Canadian salmon swim upstream, crashing and bashing over rocks, throwing themselves up waterfalls, and running the gauntlet of hungry bears looking for a free lunch just to get to the prize—the right to reproduce and be part of a generational cycle of species survival. Only those strong enough, with enough determination, will make it to the spawning grounds—where, spent of life, they will breed and, exhausted, die. The key point for reflection here is that their dream leads them straight into opposition: that is how the universe operates. Don't let anyone ever tell you it will be easy to achieve the dream. The principle of opposition to growth and change is alive and well and kicking.

Visionaries are rarely loved. More often than not they are despised, loathed and opposed. Seeing what others don't see is no guarantee of anyone's favour, even if you are trying to be helpful. When you dream, other people can't see what you see. They may think you're irrational and because they think you're mad, they may try to knock you down. Just as the salmon face innumerable hurdles in their pursuit of the dream, dreamers will always encounter opposition.

> *If you're trying to achieve there will be roadblocks.*
> *But obstacles don't have to stop you.*
> *If you run into a wall, don't turn around and give*
> *up. Figure out how to climb it, go through it,*
> *or work around it.*
> MICHAEL JORDAN, *professional basketballer*[11]

FAITH...BECAUSE IT GIVES SHARED POWER

Within an organisation a shared faith in a common vision and destiny means shared power and actually breaks down much of the inertia we see in situations where humans are working together. Fostering a shared faith in a common cause is the vital calling of leadership.

An example of a leader imparting his faith to his men can be found in the highly-acclaimed movie starring Mel Gibson, *We Were Soldiers,* based on the novel by Lieutenant-General (US

---

[11]Jordan, M. (1998) *I Can't Accept not Trying:Michael Jordan on the pursuit of excellence.* (2nd ed.). Chicago; Rare Air Media

Army Ret.) Hal Moore, *We Were Soldiers Once, and Young*. In this moving and epic tale of the early days of the Vietnam War, Hal Moore, a US Army cavalry commander shares his vision and his faith with his junior officers. He tells them that he will leave no man on the field of battle, either dead or alive, and that all will come home. Sadly, one of his young officers loses his life trying to rescue a fellow wounded soldier, and Moore blames himself for the loss of both men. In a very poignant scene, Moore (played by Gibson) says of the heroic young officer, 'He died fulfilling my promise.' **That is what shared vision and faith is all about: it gets everybody to buy into the dream, for the greater good of all.**

Let me illustrate again from mine and Debbie's experience. For our business to succeed internationally it is necessary that all of our leaders share the same level of belief in our dream. We visit some regions of the globe so infrequently that in those places success of our business depends on the key leadership. For this reason, their faith must be at least as big as ours. Because of this, when we visit the international regions, we try, above all else, to get the individual members thinking like CEOs. Chief Executive Officers know their stuff and are full of faith for what needs to happen to make a company great. We don't want our best people thinking at their current level of success. We don't want them having small kernels of faith—we want them believing what we believe, seeing what we see. Leaders need to pass on faith like red blood cells carry oxygen to the whole body, or in this case, to the whole company.

Harvey McKay, CEO of McKay Envelopes and author of *Swim With the Sharks Without Being Eaten Alive,* had the faith to position his company as number two in markets where he couldn't beat his competitors. His reasoning was that if his competitors ever fell over, didn't follow through, or failed the customer in some way, McKay Envelopes would be in position, ready to pick up the business.

McKay had the faith to keep wooing customers who showed no interest in doing business with him, and he engendered that same faith in his sales staff—while all of his competitors were telling their staff to ignore unfruitful contacts, McKay's staff were sent out to woo people who had yet to spend a penny with them. Needless to say, McKay Envelopes was a huge success story.

SHARED VISION GETS EVERYBODY TO BUY INTO THE DREAM

What do you do when a person in your team is failing? How do you treat the sales manager struggling with self-doubt? What do you do with the field manager who has lost the dream? The key task of any great leader is imparting faith—the belief that with the right level of application the dream is achievable, one small step at a time.

A shared faith means shared power. That's how the really big dreams are fulfilled. Big people are grown when they share the minds of big people. The job of any CEO or successful manager is to get his or her team thinking as he or she does, to get them dreaming like CEOs and acting on their dreams. The more people think like the big guys, the more faith there is that the dream is possible.

FOSTERING A SHARED FAITH IN A COMMON CAUSE IS THE VITAL CALLING OF LEADERSHIP

Qantas is one of Australia's most successful firms, a global brand and a business with an unsurpassed record of excellence. James Strong, former CEO of Qantas, used to hold impromptu meetings with staff at all levels of the airline. During these meetings Strong would listen to his staff, from the engineers to ground crew to baggage handlers and share his heart and his passion for the organization. Under his direction, Qantas thrived in the late 1990s. Clearly, Strong was able to get his workers thinking like CEOs. The faith he radiated—that Qantas could be a truly great airline—became everyone's faith.

The kind of energy faith brings to the dream can never be underestimated. Always remember, your dream can't expand until your faith increases.

A FEW FINAL THOUGHTS

- YOU NEED FAITH BECAUSE YOUR DREAM IS UNREAL.

- YOUR DREAM MAY BE SO UNREASONABLE IT IS TOO BIG FOR OTHERS TO SEE.

- FAITH IS A CALMNESS ... DESPITE THE OPPOSITION.

- FAITH IS A ZONE YOU GO TO WHERE YOUR BELIEF CARRIES YOU PAST DOUBT, FEAR AND INDECISION.

- ALWAYS, ALWAYS, ALWAYS BELIEVE YOU HAVE THE CAPACITY TO FULFILL YOUR DREAM.

- WHAT STOPS PEOPLE FROM SUCCEEDING IS THE WAY THEY THINK ... WHETHER THEY BELIEVE OR NOT.

- FAITH COMMUNICATED WELL SHARES POWER THROUGH THE HEART OF THE TEAM.

A winner never quits

In 1995 one of the world's most famous men woke up in a hospital bed. Some time before—he couldn't remember how long—he'd been horse riding with his wife. Everything had been fine, until ...

Now the memories all came flooding painfully back. The horse had spooked and thrown him violently down onto the rock-hard earth. That was all he remembered. But why couldn't he move his legs or arms or lift his head? And what was this strange machine controlling each laboured breath he took?

Beside his bed sat his wife, clasping his hand tenderly yet firmly, tears in her eyes. She began to explain gently about his shattered unmoving body. The machine he could hear labouring was actually pumping his lungs: he had been through massive surgery just to save his life. In the fall from the horse his spinal chord had been severed. Where once a fully functioning set of biological electronics had run straight down his spine, now a one-inch gap held it all apart, a break in the cable where no signal could pass. The man known the world over as Superman, Christopher Reeve, had proven all too human.

GIVING UP
ON DREAMS IS
WHAT FAR
TOO MANY
GOOD
PEOPLE DO

His wife Dana tried to comfort him as the reality of his situation crashed in on him. Now his life would exist only by the good graces of others and the power of machines. In desperation and depression, Reeve whispered hoarsely to his wife, 'Maybe we should let me go.' Unable to move, he no longer wanted to live. Over the ensuing months, it became clear that Christopher Reeve would need constant emotional nurture if his spirit were to survive the debilitation of his body by quadriplegia. The damage to his body seemed now to be doing irreparable damage to his will to live.

Across the globe another man sat in a mechanical chair, a man who, in his own way, had once deserved the title 'Superman'. Perry Cross, a young Australian, was just 19 in April 1994, when he was tackled in a Representative Rugby Union match and found himself at the bottom of a collapsed ruck. When the knot of players crawled back to their feet, one man lay still in a crumpled heap on the field, his nose pressed into the unforgiving earth. Perry's spine, too, had been severed.

Perry's quadriplegia meant that he could not move a muscle in his body, except for his eyelids. He could not talk, breathe, or conduct even the most basic of bodily functions. Seeing her son's desperate predicament, Perry's mum had once looked at him and asked: 'Son, should we turn this off? It's only this machine that's keeping you alive.' But his mother's tearful question only cemented a steely resolve in Perry. 'No, mum,' she could read the answer in his eyes, 'I've got too much to live for.'

Every day is a challenge for Perry Cross. He is totally dependent on the life-support chair that controls every function of his body. Three years after his accident, on a visit to the USA, Perry met Dana Reeve, who invited him to speak with her husband, Chris. Perry's travel to the USA had been a logistical nightmare, involving special airplanes and the costs of four fully paid caregivers. But on that wearying trip he sat down to lunch beside Christopher Reeve and imparted the one gift he could—the will to live. Perry Cross, quadriplegic, could be described as the man who saved Superman. Perry was living proof to Christopher Reeve that quadriplegia need not mean the end of his life.

Today Christopher Reeve and Perry Cross are friends, and both are committed to the cause of finding a permanent cure to spinal-chord severing.

Perry Cross was once a champion athlete in both Rugby Union and rowing, with a wonderful future ahead of him. All of a sudden, in 1994, his dreams of sporting glory were ripped from his grasp. Yet Perry continues to be a dreamer. He now spends his time speaking to Australian youth on the topic of suicide. Perry's message is simple: 'You kids have much more to live for than I do, yet I want to live so much. So what about you? How much do you want to live?' Everywhere he goes, Perry Cross gives to others the gift of life.

Perry's story proves that dreamers can come from anywhere and face any obstacle and overcome it. For Perry every day is a vast challenge, with enormous potential for discouragement and defeat. What gets Perry through? His commitment! Perry is committed to his dreams. He lets nothing get in his way. Perry can't breath without his ventilator; he can't even speak without a tube in his throat. The only movement he can make is to open and close his eyelids, and he has learned to sign with his eyes. Yet do you know what Perry Cross has typed on his business card? Communicator! That is a dreamer with enormous faith and commitment.

What Perry has today is a direct result of his commitment to the dream. Quitting would have been easy for Perry. Quitting is perhaps what the vast majority of people would do in his circumstances. Giving up on dreams is what far too many good people do.

But not winners.

Perhaps it is time for you to pause and reflect on your own circumstances. Next time you stall on the road to your dream because things get too tough and the price seems too high, just hold the image of Perry Cross before your eyes! Think about his example. Remember how tough life is for him and just how much he makes of it, and I guarantee whatever obstacle you are facing will look quite a bit smaller.

If you have the right vision and are prepared to pay the price, staying committed to the course despite the obstacles that arise, then, like Perry Cross, you will attain your dream.

> *I'm not just involved in tennis, I'm committed.*
> *Do you know the difference between involvement*
> *and commitment? Think of ham and eggs.*
> *The chicken is involved.*
> *The pig is committed.*
> MARTINA NAVRATILOVA,
> *former world number one tennis player*[12]

Commitment. We inevitably hit obstacles on the path to our goal. And when we do, the temptation is to quit too soon. That's why commitment is another important predetermining factor to achieving the dream.

---

[12]*International Herald Tribune* (3 Sept 1982)

Challenges to the dream usually cause stress, hardship and pain, just the things that we—as Aristotle observed—are programmed to avoid. 'Doing the hard yards' does not come naturally to humans. Yet the big dream inevitably carries a big price. Achieving the dream means tackling obstacles easily avoided by envisioning nothing more than what we currently are or have.

Any big dream will move you somewhere, demand changes of you and stretch lazy muscles. The dream is all about taking you to new places and the journey will cost in terms of travel time, trouble and energy. It is only ardent resolve that makes possible substantial, consistent progress over inhospitable terrain.

THE DREAM IS IMPOSSIBLE WITHOUT COMMITMENT

Committed dreamers hold dear four vital truths:
- A winner never quits and a quitter never wins.
- To fulfill our dreams we must have commitment.
- The dream is possible if we possess an unyielding attitude of commitment.
- Leaders have the right to lead because of their commitment.

A WINNER NEVER QUITS...AND A QUITTER NEVER WINS

Sometimes it is helpful to look at the battle to achieve the dream in the same way as a military commander would look at a war.

One thing is certain: if you start a fight, you had better be prepared to finish it. Wars are like boxing matches—won by the last person standing.

As author Konrad Adenauer once astutely observed, 'An infallible method of conciliating a tiger is to allow oneself to be eaten.' Quitters do not win battles (not with tigers nor with anyone); those with an unswerving commitment to their goals do.

During World War II, Winston Churchill inspired the disheartened English people with many of his speeches. Early in 1940, however, when British expeditionary forces stranded on the coast of France had to be withdrawn in a military volte-face, Churchill spoke honestly of what that shameful retreat meant. What he said strikes a chord with me: 'We must be very careful not to assign to this deliverance the attributes of a victory. Wars are not won by evacuations.' Although Churchill knew the evacuation was at the right option at the time he wasn't fool enough to think it would win him the war. It was still an evacuation.

Your dream is never going to be achieved if, at the first sign of a hostile force, you turn tail and flee. Quitters never, ever win and winners never, ever quit.

THE DREAM IS IMPOSSIBLE WITHOUT COMMITMENT

I don't do things halfheartedly
because I know if I do, then I can expect
halfhearted results ...
MICHAEL JORDAN, *professional basketballer*[13]

It is impossible to achieve your ultimate dream if you are prepared to settle for second best. The dream requires a commitment to excellence requiring sacrifice, hard work and a readiness to pay the price. If you are prepared to slacken your pace and swallow your own stupefying lies about the benefits of a smaller dream, you will fail to achieve the greatness you could have.

A lot of mine and Debbie's dreams are coming true today because we stayed committed. Lots of people have dreams—the trouble is, too many people lack sufficient commitment to their dreams. When it gets a little bit tough, they back out. The easy option in life is always to quit.

Debbie and I have stayed committed because we believe following our dreams brings us closer to our unique purpose as human beings. We believe every human being has a destiny waiting to be realised. Going after the dream brings those destinies a little closer to reality.

We have made a decision to be committed to each other—and in

13 Jordan, M. *I can't accept not trying: Michael Jordan on the Pursuit of excellence.* (2nd Ed). Chicago: Rare Air Media. p.13.

this commitment we have found new resolve to fulfil the dream together.

We have also remained committed to the dream because we are teachable—we are open to listening to people with greater experience than we have. When our commitment flags because of some problem or other, we get out an encouraging book, listen to a tape from a mentor or just call a friend who cares. Being teachable means we admit we don't know it all and that means we are quick to seek help from others when the going gets tough, which in turn helps keep our commitment solid.

Lastly, we have stayed committed to our passions because we are team players and we see clearly that our dreams are tied up with the desires of others. If we had quit, a lot of other people's dreams would have been affected. Above all else, we want everyone's dreams to be fulfilled.

COMMITMENT RELATES TO RIGHT THINKING

Commitment is all about right thinking. When I was keeping an eye on our marketing efforts at the Australian Grand Prix, I had no clue what life was about—I had no motivating dream. My failure to think rightly about my life—to place a large enough value on my existence—turned me into a major underachiever.

As a man thinks in his heart ... so is he ...
THE BOOK OF PROVERBS

When Debbie was first introduced to the business plan that would fundamentally alter our lives by giving us a vehicle to fulfill our dreams, we never realised how much time and effort some very unique people had invested into a personal development system to help ordinary individuals like us. Jim and Nancy Dornan, who have had an enormous influence over Debbie and myself, lavished their own resources on developing a system to grow 'big' people. They realised very early on that to grow Peter and Debbie Cox meant changing the way we thought. Jim and Nancy got us to think rightly—like the big guys, like the winners we were.

I hear a lot of corporate players these days harping on about growing sales, profits or market share, but to achieve any such worthy goals means shooting for something worthier—the growth of people. If you want to build your business, start by growing your people—in quality and in commitment to the dream!

Leadership is all about growing big people inside your organisation. Leaders should be enlargers of souls. I have seen many a man or woman entering our organisation with a shrunken visage bred of constant defeat and failure. Yet the transformation into a corporate dynamo can occur almost immediately for those offered the gifts of self-belief and self-worth. I have witnessed this many times, and I don't believe our business is unique: people are capable of anything when they possess self-esteem.

Debbie and I believe in the people we work with, with the result that their faith in themselves grows. Likewise, their performance escalates in line with their improved self-talk. All this growth stems from right thinking—on our part, and then on the part of the people we lead.

Right thinking bequeaths a winning mindset. We start to see ourselves as valuable and as having the right to our own dreams and lives of purpose. Discovering we are creatures of purpose empowers us to see meaning and value in all our attitudes and actions. That's what winners possess—a can-do attitude rooted in deep personal belief, coupled with the high net value placed on their ambitions. Winners see their dreams and ambitions as meaningful—not just for themselves, but for the advancement of all humanity.

RIGHT THINKING BEQUEATHS A WINNING MINDSET

Leaders need to see themselves as granted a very special mantle—to help other people think like winners and see themselves as high achievers. Real CEOs are not critics pouring insult after insult over divisional business plans; they are inspirers—through their words, encouragement, hand ups, and pats on the back. To inspire literally means 'to breathe into'. Inspirational leaders don't suck anything out of people; they breathe into their followers dreams, vision and belief. When leaders inspire right thinking in their staff, employees or colleagues, almost anything becomes possible in the realm of dreams.

COMMITMENT GIVES YOU THE RIGHT TO LEAD

I never particularly wanted to be a leader, but I work in a business where 90% of our organic growth is in direct proportion to the internal enlargement of people. My mentor, Jim Dornan, says it very well: 'We don't get people to grow our business; we are in the business of growing people.' With such an emphasis on people development, we have been forced into leadership roles where we become mentor, counsellor, friend, confidant and CEO, all wrapped in one.

Leadership is not about the one with the most money, the most prestige, the biggest office or the best pot plants; it is about the one with the most passion and the highest level of commitment to the dream. It is the high levels of commitment to our own dreams and to the visions of others that give us the moral right to lead.

Debbie and I firmly believe that leadership must always be ethical to have any real influence. **Nothing more rapidly undermines your moral authority than lapses of integrity.** Leaders need to be character driven, unstintingly loyal and entirely honest. These virtues will show up first in commitment to family, children and friends—these relationships are where we first learn to live out covenants: having practiced them there, we are in a position to apply what we have learnt in business and commerce. Family life is the seedbed of morally upright corporate leaders.

Commitment leads to trust. From trust, everything else flows. Commitment is the very heart and soul of the dream.

Always remember that climbing Mt Everest is a wonderful dream to have. The view is out of this world, and there can be few other experiences so emotionally powerful as that of standing on top of the world. Just remember, too, how hard a climb it is and how committed you have to be to make it all the way.

A FEW FINAL THOUGHTS

- A WINNER NEVER QUITS ... EVER.
- YOU CAN'T FULFIL A WORTHY DREAM WITHOUT BEING COMMITTED TO IT.
- COMMITMENT MEANS HAVING THE RIGHT ATTITUDE, THE PROPER FRAME OF MIND.
- COMMITMENT IS YOUR GREATEST BADGE OF HONOUR AND GIVES YOU THE RIGHT TO LEAD.
- COMMITMENT IS HANGING IN WHEN YOUR FINGERNAILS ARE TOTALLY WORN DOWN.
- COMMITMENT IS ABOUT TAKING THE THORNS WITH THE ROSES.

The most powerful force in the universe

Recently, one of my all-time heroes, Muhammad Ali, entered his sixtieth year. He is physically and mentally impaired through the progress of Parkinson's disease, an illness that has reduced the fastest feet ever to step in a ring ('float like a butterfly, sting like a bee') to a slow shuffle. But, like the winner he is, Ali remains undaunted by his physical handicap.

The man who had the nerve to declare, 'I am the greatest ...' is a true dreamer. He fought 61 professional fights for 56 wins (37 by knock out). Ali's dream was to be heavyweight champion of the world. He achieved it three times, and he did it in style. His wit is legendary: before one bout with George Foreman he famously quipped, 'I done wrassled me an alligator. I hospitalised a brick. I'm so mean I make medicine sick.' You have to be more than just a pugilist to come up with lines that good!

But Ali's dream was always enormous, much bigger than boxing. Someone once wrote of him: 'There are many men that are affected by the times in which they live but there are very few that actually shape them.' Ali has been an inspirational leader to the black communities of the world. Universally popular, Ali receives as much as US$200,000 for public appearances, all of which is generously donated to charity. He was recently quoted as saying: 'I've learned that whatever time we spend on Earth should be spent helping others and creating justice and equality for all people—not out of pity or shame, but out of love for all people with the knowledge that we belong not to many races but to one race—the human race.'[14]

Despite the challenges of his illness, Ali continues to make every day count. He is still living the dream—despite the obstacles in his way. And, as the quote above shows, his dream is energised by the most powerful force in the universe—love.

When my marriage to Debbie was in its most laughable state, I have to honestly confess I was tempted to stray. When I worked the Formula One circuit, I had numerous opportunities to do so and there were times I even told myself I would be justified because my unrequited love for Debbie hurt me so much.

Love empowered me to stay true to the dream, to be resolute in integrity. Love for myself—I wanted above all else to be able to look at myself in the mirror and to like what I saw. Secondly, love for Debbie. She was and still is my dream—how could I

---

[14] Jessup P. 'Face that opens every door.'*New Zealand Herald* (Jan 19-20, 2002). D2

abandon her? That's why I say love is the most awesome power in the universe. Love kept me focused on what was right and true within the dream.

Debbie stayed with me and I with her out of love for the dream. To regain romantic love for one another meant big changes for us as a couple, particularly on my part. A lot of those changes were enacted back in 1992 just after we began to achieve our first major successes in business. I took eighteen months out to work on my golf swing and getting myself spiritually right with God.

For me, loving the dream meant properly loving and respecting Debbie, without whom my dream would not exist. I had to learn to let Debbie have some of the limelightand, yes, I had to learn to be a man—to lead my family in a way that Debbie could respect. That meant big challenges and lots of deep, painful communication. All of that hard relational slog got us united, pulling together in the direction of our dream. Only love had the dynamic power to get us to that place.

ONLY LOVE HAD THE DYNAMIC POWER TO GET US TO THAT PLACE. ANYTHING LESS THAN LOVE AND WE WOULD HAVE FAILED

Anything less than love and we would have failed.

For stony limits cannot hold love out ...
WILLIAM SHAKESPEARE, *Romeo and Juliet, II, ii.69*

Love is a necessary ingredient in all successful dreaming. You have to love your dream. You have to show love to those who make the dream possible—to your team, employees or colleagues. Love inspires unity, which is essential to high achievement. Loving leaders inspire commitment in those who follow them.

GIVING UP ON DREAMS IS WHAT FAR TOO MANY GOOD PEOPLE DO

YOU MUST LOVE THE DREAM

When I speak of loving the dream, I am talking about something different than having fire in your belly. I am talking about being totally, 100%, sold on your dream. You can think of no higher aim or ambition in life than possession of your dream, whatever that is. If you love your dream, you will not only enjoy it, you will nurture it, care for it and resource it.

Love (in a romantic sense) is to be absolutely single-minded in your commitment, dedication and passion. In the same way that having two marital partners is considered bigamy—and not true love, at least in the Western culture—so being willing to settle for anything less than your biggest dream is not 'true love' either. Love is about singular devotion. It means making a choice to set your affections on a particular item and refusing all others. As author Adrian Henri once observed: 'Love is a fanclub with only two fans'—you and the object of your affection. Love is exclusive. So is your relationship to the dream. If you cannot say you would give everything to possess the dream, you may well have the wrong dream.

LOVE...AND REWARD SCHEMES

Incentives play a big part in contemporary life: companies offer them to employees; credit cards offer them to clients; airlines offer them to passengers. People look forward to these incentives and treat them as tokens of affirmation from those bestowing them. Consider airline reward points—a gift of appreciation to valued customers for regular patronage of an airline—who hasn't felt a little giddy when they realise they earned a free flight simply by doing what they needed to do—fly from place to place to do business? Such simple tokens of appreciation makes us feel loved and appreciated. Okay, maybe the companies offer them somewhat cynically, to keep our business, but recognition of achievement, in whatever form, is still a gift of affection. It says we are valued.

In our business, we run professional motivational conferences in which we honour those who have achieved certain results in business activity. We do this by creating a context of public acclaim and by presenting people who have excelled with small (and sometimes large) gifts. These gifts and the public recognition edify those who have achieved, and inspire hope in others that they can do the same.

Honouring those who have achieved is a practice that stems from ancient times. Ancient cultures set up statues, offered the best seats at the theatre, and even proclaimed holidays in honour of generous benefactors, sporting champions and military deliverers. Honouring good and worthy behaviour is a practice that continues in our day. Parenting experts tell us that, when raising a child, praising good behaviour works better than disciplining bad behaviour.

Sometimes we err in singling out one person over another for praise. Oskar Schindler—eulogised in Thomas Keneally's book, *Schindler's Ark* (the basis for Stephen Spielberg's inspiring film *Schindler's List*)—received very little recognition in his lifetime for his contribution to saving 1,300 Polish Jews from Hitler's holocaust in 1945. Schindler died in 1974—largely unheralded. Since the release of Keneally's story, however, Schindler has been honoured by the Jewish Holocaust Museum—Yad Vashem—as 'a righteous gentile,' and many people have been moved by his remarkable story of courage, honour and self-sacrifice.

His wife—Emilie Schindler (abandoned by Oskar in the 1950s)—died in 2001, having lived in relative obscurity in Argentina since 1949. Her last will and testament was a bitter and vitriolic biography, recently published under the title *I, Emilie Schindler*. Emilie was upset that Oskar was lauded as the saviour of so many Jews while her own contributions—which she rates as equal to his—were hardly noted. There is an important lesson here. **Success in achieving big dreams is almost always the result of many people pulling together.** Corporate goals are probably unachievable without the full commitment of all staff and employees. Praise and recognition need to be handed out accordingly and meritoriously, with no one being overlooked for the part they played.

We live in a world of global competition, just-in-time production and constant cost cutting. There is usually no fat in a well-run business—which means all hands to the wheel. But what if some of those hands don't feel as valued as they should? What if their efforts are not acknowledged? What if a boss is unable to communicate love—both for the dream and for those whose efforts help achieve the dream? How successful can the business truly be called?

How much effort or thought have you put into making your staff, employees or colleagues feel loved, valued and honoured for their efforts? Time spent here may be some of the most productive management or directional thinking any leader ever does.

LOVE INSPIRES UNITY

When Debbie and I get together with the leaders of our business (no matter where in the world they are located), there is a tremendous sense of unity. There is, in equal measure, love, respect and honour.

I believe this love and unity starts with Debbie and I being in love and totally at one. That is why I have so regularly alluded to our relationship as a couple—both its ups and downs—because I believe the principles written here were learned through loving Debbie (and in being loved by her) and, despite our troubles, in staying together. It is in the home that we have learned to practice integrity and to love others deeply and truly. And because of this success at home, we have become far more successful in fostering team spirit in a business context than we would otherwise have been. Learning to love at home has been invaluable experience for building a network and a team: you learn to be a great CEO at the hearth, not at the boardroom table.

As team leaders, our love and respect flow toward those who are helping us lead our organisation. They share our dream and live it too. If Debbie and I were to walk into leadership meetings, look people up and down as if they were untouchables and hardly exchange a word of encouragement with them, how much unity would be present? Love means embrace, warmth and sharing. That's why we so often invite our key leaders to a meal—because meals create a context for open, familiar sharing. Meals traditionally are a means of hospitality, symbolising a desire for honest, open dealings and the establishing of formal relations. In the fast-food era meals have lost some of their ritual significance; we don't tend to have the time to linger over our meals any longer, but I would suggest that we still feel embraced when someone buys us a meal. Deep in the recesses of our collective memory, we still believe a relationship has been struck by such an action.

I encourage you to have meals with your staff in your home or do something equally surprising and nurturing for them. When you show them a little love, you're on your way to growing your business and your life.

A LEADER'S LOVE INSPIRES COMMITMENT IN HIS OR HER FOLLOWERS

The love we offer our staff and colleagues inspires commitment—a commitment that is essential to achieving the dream. We need the commitment of others who are part of our dream. But people are not going to help us achieve the dream if they don't feel loved by us. How many people will continue to fight a battle if they believe their political or military masters have abandoned them? In the same way, a lack of love on our part towards our followers will result in disintegration, in the commitment and hard work required for the ultimate fulfilment of the dream.

Great coaches inspire magnificent performances from their teams. First, they get the whole team committed to each other, and then to the goal. A top-flight coach will work on creating a context of unity and love in which the team feels embraced. Team bonding is an important contributor to success at the highest levels of sport, and it is the coach's job to engineer this.

When team members feel appreciated for the vital role they play in a team, they will want to commit. As committed players they become even richer contributors to team goals. A player whose commitment is not appreciated or whose contributions are downplayed will inevitably become a poor contributor, and the team's overall performance will suffer as a result.

Great coaches are rare, but when they appear, they can be unstoppable. Sir Alec Ferguson, manager of Manchester United

PEOPLE ARE NOT GOING TO HELP US WITH THE DREAM IF THEY DON'T FEEL LOVED BY US

Football Club, has become one of the most successful sporting coaches of recent times. In the late 1990s Ferguson introduced into the team champion Dutch defender, Jaap Staam, who played a vital role as United's 'stopper' at the back. Staam's influence in the team was huge and he was a key member in the team's UEFA Champions League success in 2000. In 2001, however, Staam published a biography in which he openly mocked and spoke critically of some of the other players at Man U and the coach. Within months Alec Ferguson had exiled him to the Italian Serie A. Ferguson knows very well the coach's job is to create a context of love and unity; Staam had done a lot to undermine that unity.

Swede Sven Goran Ericksson, present coach of the English national side, is another master at creating a 'family' feel in the team and inspiring a deep commitment in his players. When Ericksson signed on, the English were perennial underachievers in Europe: their captain, David Beckham, was despised. Ericksson has since revolutionised the side's performances, and in late 2001 they even beat archrivals Germany by an unprecedented score of 5-1. Beckham has been a revelation as captain.

Ericksson has created a spirit of love and unity and nurtured a commitment to the larger team goals. **He has inspired confidence in the individual players and in the team as a whole.** That's what a great coach can do through love.

ANY DREAM
THAT IS WORTH
ACHIEVING
CAN BECOME A
REALITY WHEN
THERE IS
COMMITMENT
TO THE
PROCESS OF
FULFILMENT

Any dream that is worth achieving can become a reality when there is commitment to the process of fulfilment. But finding that commitment requires feelings of love both for the dream and for those with whom we share it.

A FEW FINAL THOUGHTS

• A FEW VERY TALENTED GUYS ONCE SAID: 'LOVE IS ALL YOU NEED'.

• LOVE IS THE ONLY EMOTION WE ARE NOT GIVEN AT BIRTH ... WE MUST BE SHOWN IT.

• IF YOU LOVE YOUR DREAM YOU'LL NURTURE IT.

• NO TEAM CAN EVER BE BUILT WITHOUT FOSTERING A SPIRIT OF LOVE, BECAUSE LOVE INSPIRES UNITY.

• LOVE INSPIRES COMMITMENT IN OTHERS.

The power of association

The great Henry Ford dreamed a dream—to create an American automotive firm (Ford Motor Company—FMC) and to bring his cars to the masses. Famous for paying his factory workers more so they could 'buy my automobiles,' Henry Ford created one of the truly great industrial powerhouses of the world.

In late 2001, Henry Ford's great-grandson—William Clay Ford—took the helm of the company in a bloodless coup, ousting Australian CEO, Jack ('Jack the knife') Nasser. William Ford is a 44-year-old Motor town maverick. He has worked for the company that bears his name for 22 years, starting out as a product-planning analyst.

Ford, the younger, is no less of a dreamer or visionary than his great-grandfather. It is his belief that one day Ford's production lines will be driven by wind power and the internal combustion engine (which drives your car but also pollutes the environment with carbon-monoxide and depletes the ozone layer) will be replaced with a fuel cell within 25 years.

Because of William Clay Ford, FMC is pursuing the Holy Grail of 'sustainable mobility', that is, the notion that cars can be built, and driven, in a way that does the least possible harm to the environment.

If you have ever visited Detroit, you will know that industrial giants like FMC have for decades been pouring waste into the Great Lakes and toxic fumes into the air. FMC may have built great cars over the years, but its reputation as a corporate citizen has been about as good as many other companies of its type—not great! What has turned a smokestack industry heir like William Clay Ford to environmentally friendly thinking?

Newspaper reports suggest that Ford's unorthodox, environment-conscious approach has not been appreciated around the family dinner table (the Ford family still owns 40% of the firm). Indeed, early in his career William was instructed to stay away from the environmental groups with whom he was so friendly. He ignored the advice!

Thanks to William Clay Ford, FMC is today 'in the vanguard of multinationals promoting environmental responsibility, human rights and corporate citizenship.' He has championed FMC's change of corporate culture despite criticisms from within that 'the company is undermining its own products.'

William Clay Ford is a dynamic example of the dream at work, and how the vitally important principle of association plays its profound role. Ford's friendships with the so-called 'green' community have revolutionised the way FMC goes after its dream of creating the best people-movers available.

There is nothing chancy about the principle of association. You choose to associate with winners or with losers, dreamers or sleepers, those who finish what they start or those who fail even to start. If you choose to pass your time with underachievers, you will join the list of 'might-have-beens'. If you associate with winners, something special will happen in your few short years on this planet. But make no mistake: the choice is yours.

The worst part of success is trying to find someone
who is happy for you ...
BETTE MIDLER, *actress, comedienne and singer*

The principle of association is central to human experience. We are community-oriented beings, creatures made for relationship. The problem is that life offers us all sorts of relationships with all types of people. Good and bad.

Some relationships become a huge asset on the road to your dream. These are the people who, out of love, unite with you in a common cause, and others who allow you to exercise your leadership over them. This 'buying in' by the many creates the team spirit and commitment I have spoken of earlier, and makes the big dream possible. Then there are the others who turn out to be obstacles, distractions, or, worst of all, downright disruptive to the pursuit of your dream.

In view of the power of association, we should observe the following rules:

- We must always seek to associate with people more successful than we are, and wiser, too.
- We should get together with like-minded people, avoiding negative types who speak against our dream.
- We must only keep company with people of high ethical character.
- We should associate with those who have a huge appetite for work.

ALWAYS ASSOCIATE WITH PEOPLE MORE SUCCESSFUL THAN YOURSELF

I once had a fantastic opportunity on an airplane flight to Los Angeles when I found myself seated beside a Fortune 500 CEO—a boss of one of the top 500 companies (as charted by

Fortune Magazine) in the USA. (Fortune 500 companies are the crème de la crème of US corporates, and their leadership teams are full of graduates from Harvard, Yale, Princeton and other Ivy League schools.)

I asked this impressive and quietly spoken gentleman what he felt was the key to his company's success.

'That's easy', he replied. 'I just hire guys brighter than myself. They make me look good.'

What humility and wisdom! You might think that highly successful individuals would fight hard to protect their patch. After all, everyone wants what leaders have achieved. But when you meet superachievers in the flesh, you soon realise how eager they are to be surrounded with people more talented than they are themselves.

As the old proverb goes, 'iron sharpens iron': spending time with people who are

YOU CAN'T ESCAPE THE INCREDIBLY POWERFUL PRINCIPLE OF ASSOCIATION smarter, more successful, wealthier and bigger dreamers than you are may be just the tonic you need to get inspired about your own situation and to start you thinking bigger.

A good friend of mine was at a business conference recently where the organisers tried to get the leaders of small-to-medium enterprises to break up into smaller groups. They thought it would be helpful to put the leaders of similarly sized enterprises together. My friend rightly complained, however, that as a leader of 5 staff himself, he would learn little from a manager of 10 staff. What he needed was time with someone who was leading 30 or more staff.

You can't escape the incredibly powerful principle of association. I believe this principle is so tried and true that you can predict the success of any individual simply by looking at the people with whom he or she associates. People will inevitably rise to the level of success (or plummet to the cellar-dweller underachievement) of their colleagues and peers.

I think a leader is ... a person who has had past
successes... and isn't afraid of taking the chance to
lead others down that road again ...
MICHAEL JORDAN, *professional basketballer*[16]

---

[16] Jordan, M. *I can't accept not trying: Michael Jordan on the Pursuit of excellence.* (2nd Ed). Chicago: Rare Air Media. p.35

In finding mentors who will stretch you, remember to look for people who know more and have done more, in terms of their people who know more and have done more, in terms of their own dream, than you have yet done in terms of your own. Ask them what they set out to do, and how they are measuring their success. The people you look for should be those who have won more often than you have won—and failed more often than you have failed.

Debbie and I are lucky to have been surrounded by so many overachievers in our business who have been extremely supportive and extremely loyal. They have told us honestly when they felt we were screwing up and they have kept us on the straight and narrow. They have been very good people with whom to associate.

> *Success isn't permanent, and failure isn't fatal …*
> MIKE DITKA,
> *former coach of the US gridiron team,*
> *the Chicago Bears*

We need to spend our time not only with people more successful than ourselves, but also with people who have earned their stripes, taken their knocks and sprouted a few gray hairs. You don't have to be old to be wise, but maturity does tend to bring sober thought and rational judgement.

No matter how far along you are on the pathway to your dream (or how successful you are), there is always someone out there wiser than yourself. Be humble enough to realise you can benefit from that person's advice and try to find a way to get time with that person.

Anthony Robins and Zig Ziglar rent themselves out by the hour for corporate coaching to some of the highest paid and most successful business people in the world. Is it because these champions of Fortune 500 boardrooms are trying to use up their expense accounts? No. It's because they recognise in Robins and Ziglar a couple of wise heads who can help them achieve even more.

Once you have received the best these wise old owls can pass on to you, however, and once you have clarified your dream and the pathway to its success, it is equally important to associate with those who will keep you on the straight and narrow.

ALWAYS ASSOCIATE WITH LIKE MINDED PEOPLE

When you receive time-tested wisdom from your 'betters,' your thinking is reoriented. Reoriented thinking needs to be reinforced. Constantly. It's all too easy to fall back into old patterns and comfortable ways of thinking and doing things.

We have found it a non-negotiable when it comes to pursuing our dream to spend time only with people who have reoriented their thinking. Our friends, our business colleagues, even the people with whom we choose to do business, must all have the mindset of dreamers. I refuse to take the risk that others will drag me back to where I was sixteen and a half years ago.

Back then, my own lack of direction was compounded by the negative influence of directionless people. When I found Debbie, I found a go-getter, someone who wanted things to be better than they were. Debbie was a dreamer and still is.

As we become clear about our dreams, we must be sure to maintain contact only with those who actually share our vision. That may sound harsh, but from one dreamer to another, you do not—I repeat NOT—want to associate with naysayers but with other visionaries.

NEVER, EVER ASSOCIATE WITH NEGATIVE PEOPLE

Negative people can be some of the most frustrating people to be around: they're like dark clouds hanging over your barbecue. Every dream you get, every passion you share and every vision you promote is immediately consigned to a metaphorical pile of rags, with throwaway lines like, 'It can't be done ...', 'Others have tried and failed ...', and 'You'll never make it ...'.

When you're dreaming you must try to aim for the biggest vision possible. **Negativity is like corrosive acid: it eats holes in**

everything. Pretty soon, your dream is a pile of metal filings a puff of wind will drive away. Negativity will kill the big dream—any dream.

Naysayers just don't get dreaming and they never seem to have any passions of their own. Not satisfied with their own mediocrity, they also want to steal your thunder—such people have no place at the dreamer's table.

Fear drives negative people to criticise the dream. But dreamers aren't fearful people; they have faith. Michael Jordan said it best—'Fear may be real to others, but to me it's an illusion.'

> *Fear is that little darkroom where*
> *negatives are developed ...*
> MICHAEL PRITCHARD, *author*

Fear is the enemy of the dream. Knowing that negativity is rooted in fear should give us the motivation to steer permanently clear of the no-can-do group.

ALWAYS ASSOCIATE WITH PEOPLE POSSESSING THE RIGHT ETHICS, ATTITUDES AND VALUES

The principle of association dictates that humans gathered together create energy and momentum. Rushing headlong into wickedness is easy when the whole crowd is going that way.

Psychologists tell us it is extremely difficult—to the point of being almost impossible—for any human to hold out against the will of a group. Our social orientation dictates that we feel better about being part of the 'in' group—even if that group is totally amoral. Just look at how many decent-enough people were swayed by the Nazis in pre-World War II Germany.

There is a famous psychological study of human beings that is both frightening—at one level—and highly encouraging, in that it shows our general tendency toward conformity to the 'in'-group perspective. Respected psychologist Solomon Asch[17] showed six people a line on a page followed by another set of three lines. The participants were then asked to say which of the other three lines was the same length as the first line they had seen. However, only one participant was genuine; the other five were 'plants'. Those five were all instructed to choose a line that obviously did not match. Very few of the 'real' participants stuck to their guns about the genuine matching line when faced with an overwhelming group opinion choosing a clearly not-matching line. In other words, it appears most people are happier to comply with the group opinion, even when it conflicts with what their own beliefs, common-sense judgement or senses might tell them. This is scary, but it also gives weight to what I am saying—you must associate with the right people.

---

[17] Asch, S.E. 'Effects of group pressure on modification and distortion of judgment' in H, Guetzkow (ed.) (1951). *Groups, leadership and men: Research in human relationships.* (Pittsburgh: Carnegie Press)

Have you heard the story of the frog helping the scorpion across the pond?

The frog asks: 'You won't sting me?'

'Of course not,' replies the scorpion with feigned piety and mock offence.

Halfway across the pond, however, the scorpion stings the frog, who, with his last dying breath, says, 'Why? Why did you do it? Now we'll both die. You, Mr Scorpion, will drown with me!'

'But,' said the scorpion, 'You must surely know: I'm a scorpion—stinging is what I do.'

If you hang around with people who like to cause trouble or with people known to 'cut a corner' or two, you will be corrupted, and you will forfeit your dream. **Find the good guys—those who believe, teach and practice the right stuff—and stick with them.**

ALWAYS ASSOCIATE WITH PEOPLE WHO HAVE A HUGE APPETITE FOR WORK

American billionaire and philanthropist John Paul Getty is reputed to have come up with the following recipe for success: 'rise early, work hard, strike oil...'

There are so many lazy people in the world not making their dreams come true that you need to be very watchful with whom you associate, lest bad character rubs off on you. The dream is an easy-to-miss target—don't show up to do the work and you are guaranteed to miss it.

If you want what you have always had, then do what you have always done. But there is a better way: surround yourself with people happy to be amongst the hard-working early birds that get the worms, and join them! Draw encouragement from them! Be inspired by them!

Believe it or not the traits of our work colleagues, business associates or partners are habit forming for us. Many studies of business settings and even sports settings show that team morale—which also includes work habits and practice regimens—generally rubs off on the whole group or team. Very few individuals will continue to swim against the tide in an organisation where discipline is slack. Most humans simply say, 'If no one else is doing the hard yards—why should I?'

The reverse is also true. Where there is a culture of hard work (and hard play afterwards), the winners will buy into the 'culture' and will contribute even more energy and generate even better results.

The Book of Proverbs contrasts the ant—a small, but industrious creature—with the sluggard or sloth, which never

IF YOU WANT
WHAT YOU HAVE
ALWAYS HAD,
THEN DO WHAT
YOU HAVE
ALWAYS DONE.
BUT THERE IS
A BETTER WAY:
SURROUND
YOURSELF WITH
PEOPLE HAPPY
TO BE AMONGST
THE HARD
WORKING EARLY
BIRDS THAT GET
THE WORMS,
AND JOIN
THEM! DRAW
ENCOURAGEMENT
FROM THEM!

BE INSPIRED BY
THEM!

does anything. In life, surround yourself with other ants—people on the team making it happen—and keep away—a long way away—from the sloths.

I doubt there has been a principle that has proven as useful to Debbie and myself as this one: associate with other dreamers. Without fail our good friends, mentors and the true believers in our dreams have been the ones to pull us up when we were wrong, to correct us when we needed it, and to affirm us in the right things. I think it is fair to say that nothing we have achieved could have been right without association with the right kind of people: people who know us, love us and want what's best for us, even when we don't want it for ourselves.

A FEW FINAL THOUGHTS

- BE CAREFUL OF THE 'IN' CROWD—ESPECIALLY IF THEY DON'T SHARE YOUR DREAM.
- IF YOU ASSOCIATE WITH NEGATIVE PEOPLE, THEY WILL CORRODE YOUR DREAM.
- FIND THE PEOPLE WHO THINK LIKE YOU— ENCOURAGE THEM, AND LET THEM ENCOURAGE YOU.
- GET A MENTOR—SOMEONE OLDER, WISER, AND A BIGGER DREAMER THAN YOU ARE.

Conclusion

For Debbie and I, the past sixteen and a half years have been one heck of a ride. The dream that started on Great Keppel has become our reality. I've gone from zero to hero in Debbie's eyes—from a guy with no dream in a dead-end job to head of my household, provider, and mentor and protector of our two boys. It's hard to believe how rocky the road once was, or to imagine how I used to feel when Debbie didn't love me. Today, we're incredibly committed to each other, and love has done that.

We are also dedicated, unequivocally, to our staff, key leaders and all the other dreamers, globally, making our business—and our life—a reality. Without them nothing would be possible. The key leaders in our business, who have achieved the same or greater levels of success than we have, are an inspiration to us,—we could not succeed without them.

We are not special cases. We have dreamed, struggled and overcome some things. We haven't yet achieved all we would like to in business or in life. And we are all too aware we have a long, long way to go still.

We want to take others with us. So we find other dreamers who are prepared to accept our love, get committed and join the program. We want these people to dream their own dreams. We want to help make their visions real. We want them to have fire in the belly, to work hard and to enjoy the ride.

YOUR DREAM IS EVERYTHING.

SO GO FOR IT!

In the past years we have achieved incredible goals and overcome untold obstacles through the destiny-transforming power of our dream. It is hard to believe that when we first envisioned it, it was as fragile as it was. Now, just sixteen and a half short years later, the dream is our reality, and every day it gets a bit richer, somewhat fuller and certainly brighter. The dream has become so enormous it literally blocks out of our heads any negative thoughts. Because we once had the guts to put the dream to the test and to prove it could be done, Debbie and I now have the faith to believe in ourselves, and to back ourselves on new dreams.

We started a business on sheer faith and determination and laboured and struggled to make it grow. Three and a half years later we retired. Here we are, fourteen years later, with product channels in over ten countries providing us with income whether we go to work or not.

Despite the fact that much of this book has focused on our story and dream, it is not ultimately about our dreams, but about yours, whatever they may be. Our wish is that in this little book you have found hope, encouragement and inspiration to identify the really big purpose for which you, a unique individual and dreamer, were placed on this earth. Whatever you want to do, it is not beyond your reach. Debbie and I are living proof of that. Your dream is everything.

So go for it!

No matter what it is! Don't let others dictate what your life can be!

You will know your dream when you discover it. You will get a passion in your gut like you wouldn't believe. The dream always comes with its own inner motivation.

As Rugby League coach Wayne Bennett suggests in his book of the same name, 'Don't die with the music in you!' Get into your dream today … while you still have a today.

You will have fun bringing your dream about because your dream will be so huge it will touch everything in your life and tickle it. No matter how hard the slog to achieve your dream, you will probably never laugh longer, louder or more often than when you finally turn your hand to whatever makes you tick.

But remember, the dream will cost you. So be ready to pay the price for your dream to become reality.

Be disciplined. Get a schedule. Be monotonously boring and repetitious about the disciplines. Plan, plan and plan some more. Review your plan. Show it to a mentor. Break it down into specific goals, and then go do the business.

Keep your integrity intact. Never, ever take a short cut to your dream. You will only shrink the dream, and yourself, in the process.

Keep having faith for your dream—the bigger your dream is, the harder it will be for you and others to see it. That does not make it any less real than something you can see.

Never, ever quit!

Love what you do and the people you do it with. That's the dream.

Associate with other dreamers and winners. Don't let a fool rob you of your dream.

Over the past few years I have watched as my grandmother lives out her days in a retirement home. She is over 90 years old, and in the twilight of her life she is surrounded by people she does not know and who don't necessarily care for her.

My own mother and father visit her three times a week. But when I go, I can hardly stand it. I only last about fifteen minutes before I have to excuse myself and leave. I find it a terribly depressing place. Don't get me wrong: I love visiting my grandmother ... but the place ... !

One evening, after one such visit, I came home and announced to Debbie, 'There's no way that when I get old, I'm going to end up in one of those places. And neither are you!'

Part of living the dream is accepting that the dream has an ending. We are none of us immortal, and time, as the old saying goes, waits for no person. You can live your dream or not (the choice is yours which road through the woods you take), but either way, you will one day have an ending. Part of the dream, then, is choosing your ending.

The end for Debbie and myself, we are determined, will not be in a dreary retirement home. After that visit, I told Debbie:

'When I die, I want to die in my retirement home, surrounded by my friends—who can change my nappy and wipe the dribble from my chin.' I don't want to die with 50 million dollars in the bank. I want to set up a foundation that owns a retirement home in perpetuity for Debbie and I, for our children and our closest friends and their children: a place where we can all go loopy together!

Come with me as I take you on a brief journey to that wondrous place. Picture this: a great iron gate, pearl white, swings open onto verdant green lawns. The road ahead is cobbled. At its end a huge white house of several stories appears. There are Corinthian columns and a huge friendly door. The front door opens onto a sparkling marble entrance hall, where staff, immaculately groomed in crisp white uniforms, usher you into motorised wheelchairs, with leather seats—in British racing green or Ferrari red. Your room is huge, with its own Jacuzzi and floor to ceiling windows overlooking the tenth tee. Are you getting the picture, feeling the power of the dream?

We'll have 14 feet by 8 feet TV screens so we can still see the football even when we're legally blind; we'll have a putting green with an automatic ball-flipper that throws the ball back out of the hole, so you don't do your back in, and our wheelchairs will be turbo-charged to move around with a 0 to 60 acceleration speed in 10 seconds or less (that should take out any remaining hair in the guys!); we'll have limousines with butlers so all the ladies can go shopping; and even if you're 82 in the shade, you'll still be allowed to wear a miniskirt if that's what takes your fancy. It's the end of the dream but you can still have fun.

In all seriousness, the bottom line is that: from old age onwards I want to be with people who love me, and who love Debbie; those who have loved and lived the dream with us. I want to grow old, totally ungracefully, together with them, having a ball because we all lived the dream. Debbie and I want to be with people who are there for each other, and we steadfastly refuse to live our last years dying in a nursing home where no one cares about us.

LOVE YOUR DREAM, LIVE YOUR DREAM AND NEVER LOSE YOUR DREAM!

That is how the dream will end. We will not take the soft option with a bucket of sleeping pills. We will live every day we are given, and keep the dream alive till it is just a small trace of an ember in the fireplace. And we will not shed one tear, and nor I hope will anyone else, when the traces of the fire go cold as they must. I hope people leave a few words on our headstones saying: The dream is everything … and it never really ends. It never did for these guys.

THE DREAM IS EVERYTHING. I WILL STAKE MY LIFE ON IT.

THE DREAM IS EVERYTHING.

Peter Cox is a dreamer and a successful global entrepreneur with product distribution in over 10 countries. Peter is a much sought after motivational speaker on leadership principles who annually speaks to tens of thousands of dreamers on almost every continent.

Forty years old, Peter has been married to Debbie for 14 years. They live in Sydney, Australia with their two sons, Dane and Jarrod.

Peter's passion is the dream ... and to continue making a difference in people's lives.